DEN NORSKE AMERII

A HISTORY OF TH

Emigration and patriotism
The period between 1905 and the outbreak of World War I in 1914 was one of the most hectic and expansive in Norwegian shipping history: in less than a decade Norway was connected with all continents through Norwegian-flag shipping services. Best-known of them all was Den Norske Amerikalinje A/S which is the official name of the Norwegian America Line. Soon to be internationally recognized by its initials NAL, the company was formally established on 27 August 1910.

Its origin has to be traced further back in history, however, namely in the emigrant traffic from Norway to the United States in the 19th. century. Before 1860, Norwegian emigrants had no alternative for the hazardous voyage across the Atlantic than by sailing vessel — a passage under cramped conditions and with no small risk of life. From the 1860s onwards, most emigrants would take a small steamer across the North Sea to England or Germany, continuing westwards with the big emigrant carriers of such well-known companies as Cunard, White Star, HAPAG, or Norddeutscher Lloyd.

It was only natural that discussion would soon arise about a direct liner service between Norway and America, preferably by a Norwegian steamship company. But sceptics argued that Norway was quite simply too small and too poor to make such a service viable, citing Peter Jebsen's ambitious, but short-lived, venture as a case in point. In 1871 Mr. Jebsen, a prominent business man in Bergen, established Det Norske-Amerikanske Dampskibsselskab (The Norwegian-American Steamship Company), offering direct regular sailings from Bergen to New York with modern, purpose-built emigrant steamers. Unsatisfactory results caused the service to be abandoned by 1876, and the vessels were re-employed in general tramp trade. A Danish company, the Thingvalla Line, was more successful with its transatlantic service which included Norway and Sweden as well as Denmark. Established in 1874, the Thingvalla Line also got into financial difficulties and was taken over in 1898 by the large Danish United Steamship Company (DFDS), which continued the services, now restyled Scandinavian American Line.

Following the dissolution of the unpopular Swedish-Norwegian Union in 1905, patriotism ran high in Norway, stimulating the public demand for a national, prestigious passenger service to America. After all, with 800,000 having left the country, Norway was second only to Ireland in the number of emigrants in relation to the total population. But the practical solutions regarding a shipping line were still complex. Arguments for and against such a line were heated, and several well-known shipowners were strongly opposed to this expensive and fool-hardy project. An inter-Scandinavian joint venture was also suggested, but the partners in question never reached a full consensus, and the project eventually came to nothing.

NAL is founded

Finally, in May 1910, plans for NAL were presented to the public, with an invitation to subscribe to a share capital of NOK (Norwegian kroner) 10 million. The first Board of Directors was elected in February 1911, and Mr. Gustav Henriksen was appointed as the first Managing Director. Later that same year, contracts for two 11,000g passenger liners were placed with Cammell, Laird & Co. Ltd., Birkenhead, for delivery in 1913.

KRISTIANIAFJORD

The two new ships were given the names KRISTIANIAFJORD and BERGENSFJORD. The "FJORD" suffix was to become the nomenclature system of the new company, a name style which was also to become widely appreciated as a symbol of Norway itself. When the two liners entered service in the spring and autumn of 1913, they became instantly successful. Passenger loads surpassed those which had been anticipated, and the flow of Norwegian travellers on the DFDS Scandinavian American Line was soon reduced to a minimum. It was clear that a third passenger vessel was required, and a contract was placed with the same British yard, for delivery in 1917. But the First World War was to intervene, and the new 13,000g vessel, named STAVANGERFJORD, was not delivered until spring 1918.

First World War

Norway remained neutral during the first World War, but was nevertheless seriously affected by the hostilities. Established trade routes were blocked, foodstuffs and other supplies from abroad were scarce, and mines and U-boats took their tragic toll of Norwegian merchant ships and sailors. It was essential for Norway to obtain a supply of grain from America, and NAL was the natural carrier. Two cargo vessels were chartered immediately in 1914, whilst two ships were purchased second-hand before the end of the year, followed by another four steamers in 1915. The demand for tonnage was so desperate that NAL even went so far as to buy a sailing-ship, the 4-masted barque AUDUN. She was used for the transportation of coal, which was in very short supply in Norway.

KRISTIANIAFJORD was lost by grounding off Cape Race in 1917, but surprisingly enough, considering the waters where NAL's vessels were trading, only one NAL vessel was lost by direct war action. At the end of the War, a dramatic fleet expansion programme was implemented. Within a short time during 1918, orders were placed with British and Canadian yards

A history of

Den norske Amerikalinje A/S
(Norwegian America Line)

1910-1995

Bjørn Pedersen and F. W. Hawks

World Ship Society
1995

CONTENTS

Den norske Amerikalinje A/S A history of the firm	5
Fleet List Notes	16
Fleet List	17
Appendix — Small Craft	78
Index	80
Acknowledgements	80

Front cover: A publicity poster of 1919

Rear cover: NOSAC STAR entering Sydney harbour, 30.1.1995 (*J. Y. Freeman*)

ISBN 0 905617 79 7

© 1995 Bjørn Pedersen and F. W. Hawks

Published by the World Ship Society
28 Natland Road, Kendal LA9 7LT England
1995

Printed by William Gibbons & Sons Ltd.,
Wolverhampton, England

Norwegian America Line

Norsk Sjøfartsmuseum

VISTAFJORD of 1973

for a total of six cargo liners, and by 1920 NAL had expanded into a large shipping company with a fleet of 12 vessels. The company also entered into the tanker business for a short period when the steam tanker FOLDENFJORD, of 10,750 dwt. was delivered in 1921. She was sold in 1928, owing to unsatisfactory results.

1920s : Expansion and problems
The two Canadian-built steamers were placed in a new service from Europe to the East coast of Canada, operated together with Canadian Pacific Ocean Services. This was a natural development from NAL's basic service to US ports. A more significant event, however, was the acquisition of the Scandinavian East Africa Line (SEAL), with four cargo steamers, in 1921. This service had been established in 1913 by shipowner Thor Thoresen, trading between Scandinavia and East Africa via Suez.

At the beginning of 1923, NAL owned 19 vessels and had grown to become one of the largest Norwegian shipping companies.

But problems were abundant. The economic collapse in the early 1920s hurt the company, and finances were strained. The new restrictive immigration laws in the United States had serious effects on NAL's westbound passenger traffic, while other companies started competing services between the USA and Scandinavia. Many of NAL's cargo vessels had to be diverted to general tramping, and the beautiful, grey-hulled NAL steamers were, for a period, to be found in all quarters of the world. In 1923, NAL also went into contract trades, when a service for the transportation of ore was established from Secondi and Takoradi in West Africa to Sauda in Norway.

The structural changes in the passenger trade to the USA forced NAL to look for alternative employment for their two passenger liners BERGENSFJORD and STAVANGERFJORD, and in 1925 the first cruises were arranged to North Cape, the fjords of West Norway, Scotland, Iceland, and the Baltic. It was a modest beginning to what would later become one of the company's most prestigious activities.

STAVANGERFJORD at North Cape   *Norsk Sjøfartsmuseum*

1930s : New ships

Prospects brightened towards the end of the 1920s, and NAL decided to build new, modern liner tonnage. Two motor vessels were ordered from AB Götaverken, Gothenburg, for delivery in 1930 and 1931. The new ships were introduced on the service to East Africa, despite the fact that the financial results from this run were far from satisfactory. The number of sailings were, in some years, reduced to just a few, even though the company started a local service in Madagascar, with small coastal vessels, in order to increase the supply of cargo.

In the mid-1930s, NAL decided that the time was ripe for another passenger liner, and a contract was made with a German yard for the 18,000g OSLOFJORD, which was delivered in 1938. The vessel was not to last for long, however, as in December 1940 she was lost by mining off the mouth of the Tyne.

OSLOFJORD

The Second World War and postwar period

While NAL's losses during the First World War were surprisingly small, the Second World War took a heavy toll on the company's fleet. In addition to two steamers, all the newly-built motor ships were lost. However, the two passenger ships BERGENSFJORD and STAVANGERFJORD survived the war. BERGENSFJORD did gallant and strenuous service as an Allied troopship, but did not return to peacetime service for NAL. STAVANGERFJORD, which had remained in Norway during the occupation, returned immediately to the transatlantic run when hostilities ended in 1945.

NAL was in desperate need of new tonnage when the Second World War was over. The first ship to join the fleet after the war was a war-built cargo liner of the C-1-A type, named FRIERFJORD. Further vessels were acquired second-hand, but newbuildings were essential, and several contracts were agreed in the immediate post-war period. Two cargo liners were ordered from Lindholmens Varv, Gothenburg, which were delivered as RANENFJORD and LYNGENFJORD in 1947, to became the first in a long line of sister vessels.

RANENFJORD *Norsk Sjofartsmuseum*

Of particular importance was the contract signed with NDSM, Amsterdam, for a new OSLOFJORD of 16,000g, which was delivered in 1949.

As mentioned earlier, NAL had been carrying shipments of ore from West Africa to Sauda since 1923, and when the war ended all the parties involved wanted to recommence the shipments. However, instead of NAL simply performing a contract of affreightment, the charterers, Electric Furnace Products Co., of Sauda, and NAL agreed to establish a separate company, A/S Malmtransport (Ore Transport Ltd.), jointly owned by NAL and the charterers. Although belonging to a separate financial entity, the Malmtransport ships were fully operated by NAL, having NAL colours and -FJORD names. Two war-built steamers were purchased second-hand and given the names VINDAFJORD (a Liberty ship) and VISTAFJORD (a Canadian-built PARK type).

Further newbuildings were added to NAL's fleet through the 1950s, and Lindholmen Varv was to deliver eight sister vessels altogether, the last one being IDEFJORD in 1960. These vessels proved suitable for the transatlantic

IDEFJORD as built

as well as the East African service. The second-hand vessels in A/S Malmtransport were sold and replaced with two newbuildings. The first of these, VINDAFJORD, was a combined ore/oil carrier — one of the first of this type in the Norwegian merchant fleet.

In 1956, a new BERGENSFJORD of 18,000g was delivered from Swan, Hunter & Wigham Richardson Ltd, Newcastle. Basically a near-sister of OSLOFJORD, she was constructed as a dual-purpose cruise vessel and transatlantic passenger liner. NAL now had three passenger liners, two of them quite new and well-suited for cruising. NAL carried an all-time record of 25,400 transatlantic passengers in 1956, but it was only a matter of time before passenger ships could no longer compete with aircraft across the North Atlantic. The fares were similar, but the difference in travelling time was indisputably not to the advantage of the ships.

BERGENSFJORD, 25.8.1966 *Michael Lennon*

1960s : Structural changes

In the early 1960s it was also clear that the cargo lines were facing profound structural changes. Containers were becoming ever more common. On its own, NAL lacked the resources needed to invest in the construction of container ships, nor was the Scandinavian trade volume to the US large enough to sustain a separate container service. Instead, NAL reverted to the less expensive alternative : to convert some of the conventional cargo vessels for pallet loading. IDEFJORD was more extensively rebuilt and also given a big crane to handle a limited number of containers. But it was all to no avail. The ships were too old, too expensive, and too cumbersome to operate in the age of containers. Nevertheless, NAL bought some second-hand conventional cargo ships as late as the mid-1960s. Two very handsome and quite large vessels were also delivered in 1960, one from Drammens Slip og Verksted and the other from Bergens mek. Verksteder. These were the first two NAL cargo liners with engines and superstructure aft.

NAL's passenger service underwent a complete metamorphosis during the 1960s, from transatlantic crossing to holidays at sea. After 45 years of transatlantic service, except for the war period, the venerable STAVANGERFJORD was withdrawn in 1963 and sold for breaking up. Her replacement, SAGAFJORD, of 24,000g was delivered in 1965, as a near-100% luxury cruise ship. In 1969, OSLOFJORD was considered surplus

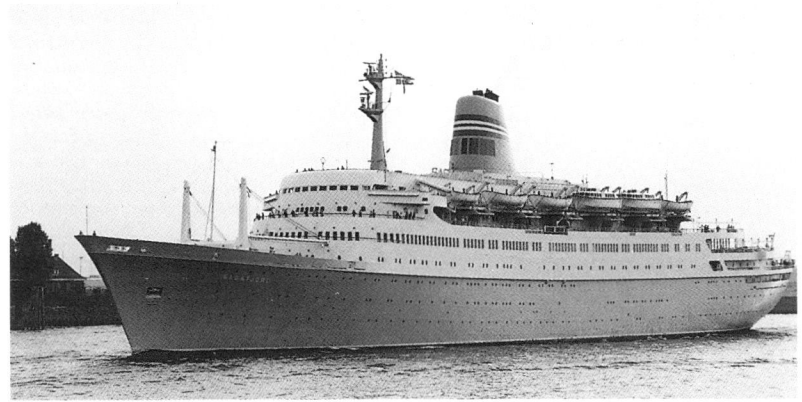

SAGAFJORD, 31.8.1979 *Joachim Pein*

to NAL's cruise programme, and the 20-year-old vessel was chartered to Linea Costa and renamed FULVIA. Unfortunately, this beautiful ship had a tragic end in July 1970, when she was gutted by fire near the Canary Islands. Luckily, all passengers and the entire crew were saved, but the burnt-out vessel heeled over and sank in deep water.

1970s : Cruises and container challenge

By 1970, NAL's passenger trade was almost solely devoted to cruises. The company's eighth and last passenger vessel was delivered in 1973. A near-sister to SAGAFJORD, the 24,300g VISTAFJORD was designed and built entirely for cruising. The only transatlantic crossings available on her were the positioning voyages between American and European cruising areas.

VISTAFJORD

However, it was clear by this time that the cruise market was also facing dramatic changes. NAL had for a long period catered primarily for the luxury sector of the cruise market, offering long voyages in great comfort for passengers willing and able to pay a correspondingly high price. The early 1970s was a period of increased competition in this segment from other Norwegian as well as foreign operators. BERGENSFJORD was no longer regarded as competitive in the top luxury market, and NAL decided to sell her in 1971.

NAL's cargo services also faced increasing problems during the 1970s. The old cargo liners were completely outdated, and the management decided to order three new vessels with modern equipment for pallets and containers as well as general cargo. These were the last cargo liners built for NAL, and proved to be very expensive and actually not as suited as expected to the markets they were to serve. After a disastrous operational loss of NOK 46 million over the three-year period 1977-79, the remaining cargo liners were chartered out, finally being sold in 1981. The service to East Africa and the Indian Ocean was still maintained, but now with chartered tonnage.

1980s : Crucial years
The period 1980 to 1984 became crucial for NAL. The company went through great organisational and structural changes, and it was a period where one tried to "save the crumbs" by an effort to rebuild the company through new activities. The two cruise vessels were transferred to a new company, Norwegian American Cruises A/S (NAC) in 1980, a joint venture on a 50/50 basis with Leif Høegh & Co.

VINDAFJORD   *W.S.P.L. Slide collection*

For the East Africa/Indian Ocean service, NAL now chartered three large RoRo vessels which were given traditional NAL names: VINDAFJORD, NOREFJORD, and KONGSFJORD. However, this venture became NAL's last effort in this trade, as the entire liner service was closed down at short notice, and the chartered ships were either relet or returned to their owners. The remaining assets in the East Africa service were sold in 1981 to a subsidiary of Deutsche Afrika Linie. NAL's financial problems forced the company to sell its prestigious head office in central Oslo. Other land-based activities such as a forwarding company, a brokerage company, properties in Madagascar, and a mountain hotel were also disposed of.

Ownership of NAL also changed dramatically through this brief, fateful period. The largest shareholders in NAL, Leif Høegh & Co., sold their shares, and in 1982 the controlling ownership was shared between the Andenæs

Group and Platou Investment A/S. At the beginning of 1983 there were no owned vessels left in the NAL fleet, only timechartered RoRo ships that were to be redelivered to their owners later that year. But NAL still had a small positive balance of cash.

Product carriers and new owners

At the end of 1983 a new investment company was established by NAL named K/S NAL Bulk Shipping A/S, to charter a product carrier building in Japan. The vessel was delivered in 1984 and named BERGENSFJORD. The charter period was 10 years, with a purchase option for NAL. Later on, 50% of the ownership of this K/S company was sold to Investa. A second product carrier was also chartered on similar terms and given an NAL name — OSLOFJORD. Sad to say, the results from these charter parties did not bring the company much profit. The accounts for 1984 resulted in a loss, while the value of the ships remained weak, and the charter parties for BERGENSFJORD and OSLOFJORD were sold in 1985.

The Andenæs and Platou groups sold their NAL shares to Herness Shipping in the same year, but in May 1986 Herness Shipping sold out to A/S Poseidon. NAL still had several part-ownership investments in other vessels. The largest of these were 26% in the 30,000 dwt chemical carriers STOLT VINCITA and STOLT VENTURA, and 62% ownership in VIRA GAS, a 12,000 cbm gas carrier. However, the market value of this tonnage fell dramatically in the spring of 1986. NAL's share capital got into deficit, and the company was forced to restructure and re-finance. All assets were sold, and after the restructuring the company's long-term debt was redeemed.

By this time, the goodwill which had traditionally been associated with the company name was probably the major asset of any value still left of NAL. The share capital was written down to only 10% of the original value and later increased again by direct share issues. Poseidon A/S sold their share majority to Fearnley & Eger A/S in December 1986.

NAL, Øivind Lorentzen A/S and NOSAC

New business was secured by NAL's purchase of the two car carriers NOSAC MASCOT and NOSAC BARBRO from Arth. H. Mathiesen. The vessels were on a bareboat charter to K/S Benargus A/S & Co. which was owned by Øivind Lorentzen A/S, Oslo, managers of the automobile transportation pool Norwegian Specialized Autocarriers (NOSAC in abbreviation). The strategy of NAL was further to develop interests in the car carrying business.

NOSAC BARBRO, 15.8.1986   *Michael Lennon*

Fearnley & Eger had at that time four car carriers in operation, and NAL and Fearnley & Eger saw that the ownership and control of the two newly acquired vessels could be further enhanced by investment into Øivind Lorentzen A/S. In June 1987, NAL offered to take over all shares, assets, and employees of Øivind Lorentzen A/S. Agreement was reached in July with accounts for the acquisition to be effective as from 1 January 1987. The takeover price was NOK 480 million, to be settled and paid as on 1 September 1987. Øivind Lorentzen thus became a subsidiary of NAL, but the two companies were amalgamated during the summer of 1988.

The purchase of Øivind Lorentzen A/S was made possible through an increase of the NAL share capital to NOK 95 million, convertible loans of NOK 69 million and NOK 100 million, as well as the use of NAL's own resources. Through this purchase NAL became a 50% pool partner in NOSAC. The other partner is Wilh.Wilhelmsen Ltd. A/S. The vessels previously owned and controlled by Øivind Lorentzen A/S were now incorporated into NAL's fleet. Fearnley & Eger now reduced their shareholding of NAL to 35%, which was increased to 50% during 1990.

Øivind Lorentzen A/S was another of the shipping companies with roots back into the pioneering years of Norwegian liner services. In 1914 Mr. Lorentzen, one of Norway's foremost shipping personalities, took delivery of BRAZIL, the first ocean-going motor vessel in the Norwegian fleet. Built for a competitive liner service to Brazil, she was immediately resold to Fred. Olsen, one of the partners in the newly- established Norwegian South America Line, while Mr. Lorentzen became the first managing director of the Line. In 1936, Øivind Lorentzen established his own liner service, NOPAL Line, between North and South America. During the Second World War he served as director of Norway's Allied merchant fleet, Nortraship. NOPAL Line continued after the war, while Øivind Lorentzen A/S also ventured into new activities: gas transportation, bulk trade, and, from 1972, car carrying.

NOSAC RANGER loading cars

NOSAC was based on contracts for shipment of Japanese cars to Europe. The service and the fleet of carriers were steadily expanded during the 1970s, but when the company obtained a large contract with General Motors for carrying cars from Japan to the USA in 1983, further vessels and capital were required. A car carrier pool was formed between Øivind Lorentzen A/S and Wilh. Wilhelmsen Ltd. A/S on a 50/50 basis, and a number of vessels were contracted for delivery between 1985 and 1987. Through the sale by Wilh. Wilhelmsen Ltd. A/S towards the end of 1988 of two of their vessels to K/S Benargus A/S & Co. NAL obtained 70% of the pool partnership. NOSAC had now become the main activity of NAL and a very profitable one as well. The names of the vessels were NOSAC TASCO and NOSAC TANCRED, now renamed NOSAC EXPLORER and NOSAC SEA respectively.

In November 1988, NAL acquired the second-hand car carrier TARGET. Although this vessel was operated outside the NOSAC pool, the purchase was nevertheless a step towards further involvement in the car carrying trade.

Trinity Bulk Carriers (TBC) — a passing incident

1989 turned out to be the best year ever for NOSAC, with correspondingly positive results for NAL — a profit of NOK 149 million. This year also brought about a new business area for NAL — diversification into handy-size bulk carriers. In May 1989, NAL and China Foreign Trade Transportation (Sinotrans), Beijing, jointly formed Sinor Shipping Inc. Each partner had a 50% ownership, and tonnage was obtained through chartering. In order further to strengthen its bulk shipping engagement NAL acquired 50% of Trinity Shipping A/S — another new handy-size bulk carrier charter operator. Finally, NAL established a wholly-owned company, K/S NALBulk, to bareboat charter for ten years a handy-size bulk carrier which was renamed KRISTIANIAFJORD.

NAL further expanded their bulk activities in the following year by initiating the establishment of Trinity Bulk Carriers A/S (TBC) as a joint chartering pool with 33 1/3 % participation. The other partners were Sinotrans (China) and Mitsui-OSK Lines. Each partner was to operate five handy-size bulkers in the pool. A second handy-size bulk carrier was chartered on a 10-year bareboat charter party with purchase option. Named KONGSFJORD, the vessel was fully included in NAL's fleet, but operated in TBC. The expansion in this trade continued in the following year when a third bulker was purchased and renamed NOREFJORD. The TBC pool now had reached its tonnage aim, each partner having five vessels in the pool, with five to ten additional vessels on voyage basis or time charter.

During 1990 it also became clear that the majority shareholders of NAL — Fearnley & Eger A/S — were having serious financial problems due to heavy operating losses and dramatic falls in ship values. By mutual consent it was agreed that NAL would acquire the Fearnley & Eger A/S interest in five car carriers through their shares in different independent limited partnership companies. The vessels in question were FERNGOLF, FERNPASSAT, KASSEL,

KASSEL in 1987 *Fotoflite incorporating Skyfotos*

BRAUNSCHWEIG, and FERNSTAR. These vessels were subsequently taken over by NAL management and part-ownership and operated outside the NOSAC pool. FERNSTAR, renamed LANE, came to a tragic end in that same year, when she collided with another car carrier outside Gibraltar and sank. During the summer of 1991, Fearnley & Eger's shares were sold to three different investment groups, Astrup Fearnleys, Kværner Group and Vital Insurance.

In 1993, the Board of Directors decided to divest NAL of its bulk carrying investments, and to reduce commitments as soon as practicable: the bulk activities contained in TBC had resulted in a loss of NOK 19 million for the company, and NAL's interest in TBC was sold as well as the bulk carrier NOREFJORD. Also the bareboat charters of KRISTIANIAFJORD and KONGSFJORD were cancelled. During 1994 the bareboat charters of the remaining bulk vessels TRINITY SEA and TRINITY STAR were cancelled.

The current strategy of NAL is to concentrate on RoRo and car carrying business through NOSAC. In 1994, NOSAC and its two partners accepted the invitation to purchase 50% of the ownership of SKAUKAR (ex NOSAC SKAUKAR when on charter to NOSAC from B. Skaugen Shipping A/S). Wallenius Lines, Stockholm, had exercised their purchase option for the vessel, which they had renamed FIDELIO, and wanted NOSAC to take a 50% share in the vessel for operation under the American flag. The 50% share for NOSAC was divided 35% to NAL and 15% to Wilh. Wilhemsen Limited AS.

In the early autumn of 1995, the three main shareholders in NAL — Fearnley's, Kvaerner and Vital — sold their shares, and the main shareholders are now Bergesen D.Y. Group and the Wilh. Wilhelmsen Limited Group.

Epilogue

Having successfully braved its near-death experience a decade ago, NAL is now as vital and active as ever before in its 84 years of operation. Today's involvement in worldwide car carrying is a far cry from transatlantic passenger and cargo liner trades. But survival is also a question of the ability to adjust to changes, and the fact that NAL is doing well and is likely to do well in the foreseeable future, must be considered proof of flexibility and adaptability.

FLEET LIST NOTES

In the Fleet List the number preceding the name is the ship's chronological number in the NAL fleet.

If more than one ship of a particular name has featured in the fleet "(1)" "(2)" etc. follows the name to show whether she is the first, second, etc. to bear that name. The dates following the names are those of entering and leaving the fleet and, if the ship has borne more than one name whilst in NAL service, the dates when she bore those names.

Tonnages can vary during the life of a ship and those given are taken from a representative volume of "Lloyd's Register", as are the dimensions. For ships up to number 52 these are the registered length x beam x depth in feet and tenths, from 53 to 67 the overall length x beam x draft in feet and inches, and from 68 onwards the length between perpendiculars (with the overall length in brackets) x extreme breadth x moulded depth in metres, plus the draft.

Oil engines are Two or Four stroke cycle (2S.C. or 4S.C.) single acting (SA) or double acting (DA) and the type (e.g. "Burmeister & Wain") is given where it is not of the manufacturers' own design.

The ships' histories are corrected up to October 1995.

FLEET LIST

KRISTIANIAFJORD — *Norsk Sjøfartsmuseum*

1. KRISTIANIAFJORD (1) (1913-1917) Passenger ship
Tonnages: 10,669 gross, 6,496 net.
Dimensions: 512.1 x 61.2 x 29.4 feet.
Machinery: Two four cylinder quadruple-expansion steam engines by the shipbuilders, driving twin screws.
Passengers: 104 1st. Class, 232 2nd. Class, 762 3rd. Class.
23.11.1912: Launched by Cammell Laird & Co. Ltd., Birkenhead (Yard No. 784) for NAL. *5.1913:* Delivered. *15.6.1917:* Ran aground on Mistaken Point near Cape Race, Newfoundland, due to a navigational error, while on a voyage from New York to Bergen, via Halifax, with 1,144 passengers and crew and 3,740 tons of general cargo. All on board were saved by the ship's own lifeboats. *28.7.1917:* Wreck destroyed during a storm before it could be refloated.

BERGENSFJORD — *Norsk Sjøfartsmuseum*

2. BERGENSFJORD (1) (1913-1946) Passenger ship
Tonnages: 10,666 gross, 6,475 net.
Dimensions: 512.4 x 61.2 x 29.4 feet.
Machinery: Two four cylinder quadruple-expansion steam engines by the shipbuilders, driving twin screws.
Passengers: 105 1st. Class, 216 2nd. Class, 760 3rd. Class.
8.4.1913: Launched by Cammell Laird & Co. Ltd., Birkenhead (Yard No. 787) for NAL. *9.1913:* Delivered. *1921:* Tonnages became 10,709 gross, 6,448 net.

1926: Tonnages became 11,013 gross, 6,406 net. *1930:* Tonnages became 11,015 gross, 6,550 net. *1932:* Fitted with two low-pressure steam turbines. *15.4.1940:* Laid up on arrival at New York from Oslo, as Norway had been invaded by German forces. *11.1940:* Requisitioned by the Ministry of War Transport (UK), and converted to a troopship at Halifax, Nova Scotia. By the end of the war, the ship had carried a total of 165,000 troops, sailed 300,000

BERGENSFJORD on war service   *A. Duncan*

miles, and been at sea for 919 days. *2.1946:* Chartered for one voyage to carry GI brides from Europe to the United States, and then returned to NAL. *8.1946:* Sold to Panamanian Lines Inc. (Fratelli Cosulich, Trieste, managers), Panama and renamed ARGENTINA for emigrant traffic from Italy to South America. *1949:* Owners restyled Mediterranean Lines Inc., Panama (same managers). *1952:* Sold to Home Lines Inc., Panama. *1953:* Sold to Zim Israel Navigation Co. Ltd., Israel, and renamed JERUSALEM for Israel/New York service. *1957:* Renamed ALIYA for Israel/Marseilles service. *13.8.1959:* Arrived at La Spezia for breaking up.

3. TRONDHJEMSFJORD (1) (1914-1915)
Tonnages: 4,248 gross, 2,737 net, 7,500 deadweight.
Dimensions: 380.0 x 49.0 x 26.4 feet.
Machinery: Three cylinder triple-expansion steam engine by North Eastern Marine Engineering Co. Ltd., Newcastle.
21.12.1911: Launched by Northumberland Shipbuilding Co. Ltd., Newcastle (Yard No. 185) as COTSWOLD RANGE for Neptune Steam Navigation Co. Ltd., Liverpool, (Furness, Withy & Co. Ltd., managers). *3.1912:* Delivered. *23.12.1914:* Bought by NAL and renamed TRONDHJEMSFJORD. *28.7.1915:* Stopped by the German submarine U 41 in a position 61.08 N, 03.27 W while on passage from New York to Bergen with general cargo. Crew and 4 passengers took to the lifeboats, and the ship was then torpedoed. The lifeboats were towed by the submarine until the occupants could be transferred to the Norwegian sailing vessel GLANCE which landed them at Helsingborg.

4. DRAMMENSFJORD (1) (1914-1924)
Tonnages: 4,338 gross, 2,755 net, 7,500 deadweight.
Dimensions: 380.0 x 49.0 x 26.4 feet.
Machinery: Three cylinder triple-expansion steam engine by Richardsons, Westgarth & Co. Ltd., Sunderland.

DRAMMENSFJORD *Norsk Sjøfartsmuseum*

12.1911: Completed by Northumberland Shipbuilding Co. Ltd., Newcastle (Yard No. 187) as CHILTERN RANGE for Neptune Steam Navigation Co. Ltd., Liverpool, (Furness, Withy & Co. Ltd., managers). *12.1914:* Bought by NAL for £45,000 and renamed DRAMMENSFJORD. *1924:* Sold to Turnbull Coal & Shipping Co. Ltd., Cardiff, for £32,000 and renamed RAISDALE. *1933:* Owners became Turnbulls (Cardiff) Ltd. *1933:* Sold to L. A. Embiricos, Greece, for £5,000 and renamed RINOS. *1936:* Sold to Muir Young Ltd., London. *1937:* Sold to V.K.Song, China, and renamed YONG SHYANG. *1938:* Captured by the Japanese, taken over by Kyodo Kaiun K.K., Japan, and renamed EISYO MARU. *5.6.1940:* Sank after collision in a position 42.20 N, 140.55 E while on passage from Muroran to Tokio.

FRIERFJORD *Norsk Sjøfartsmuseum*

5. FRIERFJORD (1) (1915-1921)
Tonnages: 941 gross, 571 net, 1,125 deadweight.
Dimensions: 201.2 x 30.2 x 12.5 feet.
Machinery: Three cylinder triple-expansion steam engine by the shipbuilders.
4.1897: Completed by Akers Mekaniske Verksted, Kristiania (Yard No. 167) as SALAMANCA for Otto Thoresen A/S, Kristiania. *1911:* Sold to Northwich

Carrying Co. Ltd., Liverpool, and renamed MAY. *1911:* Sold to N. Bugge, Tønsberg. *1911:* Sold to D/S Tresfonds Rederi (Sigval Bergesen, manager), Stavanger and renamed TRESFOND. *1913:* Owners became D/S Langfonds A/S (same manager). *1915:* Bought by NAL and renamed FRIERFJORD. *1921:* Sold to D/S A/S Gudrun (L. Andersen, manager), Tønsberg and renamed GUDRUN. *1927:* Sold to A/S Nor (Halvor Kongshavn, manager), Haugesund. *27.7.1927:* Driven aground near Tamatave, Madagascar during a storm when arriving from Mauritius with general cargo.

ROMSDALSFJORD   *Norsk Sjøfartsmuseum*

6. ROMSDALSFJORD (1915-1920)
Tonnages: 4,580 gross, 3,242 net, 7,500 deadweight.
Dimensions: 355.5 x 50.0 x 27.6 feet.
Machinery: Three cylinder triple-expansion steam engine by Palmers' Shipbuilding & Iron Co. Ltd., Newcastle.
3.1908: Completed by Robert Stephenson & Co. Ltd., Hebburn (Yard No. 113) as DORINGTON COURT for Cressington Steamship Co. Ltd. (Haldinstein & Co. Ltd., managers), London. *1912:* Sold to Skibs-A/S Per Gjerdings Rederi, Bergen, and renamed VALLY. *1914:* Owners became A/S D/S Vally (Per Gjerding, manager), Bergen. *1915:* Bought by NAL and renamed ROMSDALSFJORD. *9.12.1920:* Wrecked off Sambro Island, Nova Scotia, while on passage from Narvik to Halifax and Baltimore with ore.

TANAFJORD in war-time   *Norsk Sjøfartsmuseum*

7. TANAFJORD (1) (1915-1920)
Tonnages: 4,513 gross, 2,835 net, 6,750 deadweight.
Dimensions: 350.0 x 47.7 x 19.5 feet.
Machinery: Three cylinder triple-expansion steam engine by Sir C. Furness, Westgarth & Co. Ltd., Middlesbrough.
24.9.1900: Launched by Sir Raylton Dixon & Co. Ltd., Middlesbrough (Yard No. 474) as CASTANO for Atlantic & Eastern Steamship Co. Ltd. (J. Glynn & Son, managers), Liverpool. *1910:* Sold to M.M. de Arrotegui, Spain. *1915:* Bought by NAL and renamed TANAFJORD. *1920:* Sold to Peder Kleppes Rederi A/S (Peder Kleppe, manager), Bergen, and renamed HALLBJØRG. *1922:* Sold to Forenede Rederi A/S (Gørrissen & Co. A/S, managers), Kristiania and renamed EKSJØ. *1924:* Sold to D/S A/S Erle (Fearnley & Eger, managers), Oslo. *26.6.1926:* Arrived at Stavanger for scrapping by Skipsopphugging Co., Stavanger.

LYNGENFJORD in war-time   *Norsk Sjøfartsmuseum*

8. LYNGENFJORD (1) (1915-1924)
Tonnages: 5,097 gross, 3,171 net, 7,820 deadweight.
Dimensions: 390.0 x 52.0 x 27.0 feet.
Machinery: Three cylinder triple-expansion steam engine by D. Rowan & Co., Glasgow.
16.4.1903: Launched by Napier & Miller Ltd., Glasgow (Yard No. 128) as KERAMIAI for C.S. & A.S. Vagliano, Greece. *6.1903:* Delivered. *1907:* Owner became A.S. Vagliano, Greece. *1915:* Bought by NAL and renamed LYNGENFJORD. *1924:* Sold to H.M. Wrangell & Co. A/S, Haugesund and renamed SIGRUN. *1929:* Sold to F.N. Nordbø, Haugesund, rebuilt as a herring oil factory ship (5,153 gross, 3,150 net), and renamed NORSKEHAVET. *1930:* Taken over by Norsk Sildeindustri A/S (H. M. Wrangell & Co. A/S, managers), Haugesund. *1936:* Sold by compulsory auction to H. M. Wrangell & Co. A/S, Haugesund. *1937:* Sold to I/S Norskehavet (Bj. Gundersen, manager), Haugesund. *1937:* Sold to Skibs-A/S Ringulv (Olav Ringdal, manager), Oslo and renamed RINGULV. *1937:* Rebuilt as a cargo ship (4,702 gross, 3,150 net). *17.6.1940:* Interned at Oran, later seized by the Vichy French authorities. *1941:* Renamed STE. MARTHE. *11.1942:* Taken over by the German Kriegsmarine. *14.6.1943:* Torpedoed and sunk in the Straits of Messina by H.M. Submarine UNITED.

9. LILLEFJORD (1) (1916-1920)
Tonnages: 383 gross, 212 net, 480 deadweight.
Dimensions: 136.6 x 23.1 x 16.5 feet.
Machinery: Two cylinder compound steam engine by the shipbuilders.
1.1896: Completed by A. G. Neptun, Rostock (Yard No. 153) as BÜRGERMEISTER MASSMANN for Nordische Dampfschifffahrts A.G (F. Petersen, manager), Germany. *25.10.1899:* Sold to Michael Jebsen, Germany, and renamed EMMA. *24.1.1900:* Sold to Deutsche Dampfschifffahrts Gesellschaft "Kosmos", Germany, and renamed KOSMOS. *1903:* Sold to Hamburg-Südamerikanische Dampfschifffahrts Gesellschaft, Germany, renamed COLUMBUS, and registered at Buenos Aires (Argentine flag) for Argentine coastal service. *3.1911:* Sold to Chr. Salvesen & Co., Leith, for inter-Island services in the Falkland Islands. *5.1914:* Sold to Thor E. Tulinius, Iceland (Danish flag). *22.8.1914:* Renamed ISAFOLD. *28.12.1915:* Sold to A/S Frederiksen & Moller, Mandal. *1.1916:* Bought by NAL and renamed LILLEFJORD. *1920:* Sold to Bodø D/S A/S (Magnus Fische, manager), Bodø. *1921:* Renamed BØRVASTIND. *1923:* Sold to D/S A/S Risøy (M. Clausen, manager), Haugesund, and renamed RISØY. *22.1.1926:* Foundered in stormy weather west of Jæren while on a voyage from Aalesund to Ostend with a cargo of herring.

AUDUN in war-time   *Norsk Sjøfartsmuseum*

10. AUDUN (1916-1919) 4-masted barque
Tonnages: 2,018 gross, 1,891 net.
Dimensions: 285.2 x 40.5 x 23.8 feet.
24.3.1887: Launched by A. Stephen & Sons Ltd., Glasgow (Yard No. 302) as ARMADALE for J. & A. Roxburgh, Glasgow. *8.1909:* Sold to A/S Audun (Jens Marcussen, manager), Risør, and renamed AUDUN. *7.1916:* Bought by NAL. *3.1919:* Sold to A/S Almora (A.H.Torbjørnsen), Tønsberg. *1923:* Sold to Petersen & Albeck, Copenhagen, for breaking up.

11. RANENFJORD (1) (1917-1933)
Tonnages: 5,404 gross, 3,464 net, 7,850 deadweight.
Dimensions: 383.3 x 50.0 x 25.8 feet.
Machinery: Three cylinder triple-expansion steam engine by the shipbuilders.
4.1908: Completed by Union Iron Works, San Francisco (Yard No. 86) as ISTHMIAN for American-Hawaiian Steamship Co., USA. *1917:* Bought by NAL

RANENFJORD

and renamed RANENFJORD. *1933:* Sold to A/S Krogstads Dampskibsrederi II (Alf L. Ombustvedt, manager), Oslo, and renamed NIDARHOLM. *3.1934:* Sold at Avonmouth to Metal Industries Ltd. for £5,500. *14.3.1934:* Arrived at Rosyth for breaking up. *10.10.1934:* Demolition commenced.

STAVANGERFJORD in war-time (1918)

12. STAVANGERFJORD (1918-1964) Passenger ship

Tonnages: 12,977 gross, 7,527 net.
Dimensions: 532.5 x 64.2 x 29.3 feet
Machinery: Two four cylinder quadruple-expansion steam engines by the shipbuilders, driving twin screws.
Passengers: 88 1st. Class, 318 2nd. Class, 820 3rd. Class.
5.1917: Launched by Cammell Laird & Co. Ltd., Birkenhead (Yard No. 821).
2.1918: Delivered to NAL. *1926:* Tonnages became 13,156 gross, 7,793 net.
1932: Fitted with two Bauer Wach low-pressure turbines by A. G. "Weser", Bremen. *12.1939:* Laid up in Oslo. *20.9.1940:* Requisitioned by the German Kriegsmarine. Planned to be rebuilt as a hospital ship, but the rebuilding was not carried out, and the vessel remained at the berth in Oslo as a troop depot

STAVANGERFJORD with the shorter funnels fitted in 1937

ship. *21.2.1945:* Returned to NAL. *1948:* Tonnages became 13,304 gross, 7,667 net. *1951:* Tonnages became 13,334 gross, 7,497 net. *1959:* Tonnages became 14,015 gross, 7,818 net. *14.12.1963:* Arrived at Oslo on her last Atlantic crossing. *1964:* Sold for scrapping, and *4.2.1964:* arrived at Hong Kong, under her own power, for breaking up by Patt, Manfield & Co. Ltd. *3.1964:* Demolition commenced.

13. IDEFJORD (1) (1919-1921) / LILLEFJORD (2) (1921-1923)
Tonnages: 147 gross, 80 net, 180 deadweight.
Dimensions: 96.7 x 21.1 x 8.0 feet.
Machinery: Single acting oil engine by N.V. Kromhout Motorenfabriek, Amsterdam.
5.1914: Completed by Kaldnæs Mekaniske Verksted, Tønsberg (Yard No. 34) as ERIK ASK for Erik Stensrud, Skien. *1915:* Sold to A/S Transit (A. Johnsen, manager), Skien, and renamed UNION V. *1916:* Sold to Ingolf Bjørnstad, Bergen. *1917:* Sold to Arendal Smelteverk, Arendal, and renamed STORENG. *1919:* Sold to A/S Transit (A. Johnsen, manager), Skien. *1919:* Bought by NAL and renamed IDEFJORD (the first motor vessel in the NAL fleet). *1921:* Renamed LILLEFJORD. *1921:* Fitted with a four-cylinder oil engine manufactured by Lysekil Mekanisk Verksted A/B, Lysekil. *12.1923:* Sold to Eskilstuna Nya Rederi A/B, Sweden, and renamed TUNA. *1925:* Machinery replaced by a two-cylinder compound steam engine manufactured in 1897 by A/B Lindholmen-Motala Varv, Motala. *3.1946:* Sold to Einar Lundgren, Sweden. *18.11.1946:* Ran aground in Tjuvholmssundet, north of Läckö, in Lake Vänern, and sank in 8 metres of water. Cargo was cement in sacks. *1947:* Wreck taken over by Försäkrings-A/B Fylgia, Stockholm. *2.1947:* Wreck sold to John Sörman, Stockholm. *21.6.1947:* Salvage work started. *19.7.1947:* Vessel refloated and towed to Karlstad Varv for repairs. Machinery replaced by a new oil engine manufactured by Lysekil Mekanisk Verksted A/B, Lysekil. *5.1948:* Sold to Rederi-A/B Robur (Gösta Hörgren, manager), Sweden. *5.1951:* Sold to Fritz Hilding Bergestedt Partrederi (Gösta Hansson, manager), Sweden. *1955:* Owners taken over by Anders Karlsson Partrederi, Sweden. *1.1957:* Sold to Helge Källsson (Erik Thun A/B, managers), Sweden. *1961:* Sold to Partrederiet för m.s TUNA (A/B Aug. V. Svensson, managers), Sweden. *9.1964:* Sold to Gösta Johansson, Sweden. *1977:* Owners became Gösta Johansson Partrederi, Sweden. *3.1977:* Sold to Carlos Gumbs, Netherlands Antilles (registered under the Cyprus flag). *1995:* Reported still in service.

NOREFJORD Norsk Sjøfartsmuseum

14. NOREFJORD (1) (1921-1949)
Tonnages: 3,082 gross, 1,917 net, 5,500 deadweight.
Dimensions: 331.7 x 46.7 x 23.1 feet.
Machinery: Three cylinder triple-expansion steam engine by North Eastern Marine Engineering Co. Ltd., Newcastle.
Laid down as WAR GLADE for The Shipping Controller, London.
11.9.1919: Launched by Wood, Skinner & Co. Ltd., Newcastle (Yard No. 214) as NOREFOS for Skibs A/S Thor Thoresens Linje (Otto & Thor Thoresen, managers), Kristiania. *1.1920:* Delivered. *1921:* Bought (as part of Skandinaviske Øst-Afrika Linje) by NAL and renamed NOREFJORD. *1949:* Sold to F. N. Nordbø A/S, Haugesund, and renamed RYVARDEN. Later registered in the name of A/S Ryvarden (F. N. Nordbø, manager). *1953:* Laid up at Haugesund. *Later in 1953:* Sold to Rolf Wigands Rederi, Bergen. *1955:* Sold to Halvorsen Shipping Co. A/S, Bergen. *1958:* Sold to Pan Norse Steamship Co. S.A., Panama, and renamed NORSE LADY. *14.8.1958:* Ran aground near Parigi, Celebes. *16.8.1958:* Seized by Indonesian rebels, who got her afloat and took her to Belang, where she was beached. *18.8.1958:* Ship sighted by the Indonesian Navy. *22.8.1958:* Set on fire by shelling, and totally burnt out. *3.1966:* Wreck sold to Hong Kong buyers, and sold on to Taiwan shipbreakers for scrapping. *3.1966:* Arrived at Kaohsiung.

FOLDENFJORD Norsk Sjøfartsmuseum

15. FOLDENFJORD (1) (1921-1928) Tanker
Tonnages: 7,277 gross, 5,054 net, 10,570 deadweight.
Dimensions: 430.4 x 59.3 x 33.3 feet.
Machinery: Three cylinder triple-expansion steam engine by the shipbuilders.
12.5.1921: Launched by Sun Shipbuilding Co., Chester, Pennsylvania (Yard

No. 44) for NAL. *1928:* Sold to Petroleum Securities Co., USA, and renamed LARRY DOHENY. *1933:* Sold to Richfield Oil Co. (subsequently Richfield Oil Corp.), USA. *23.12.1941:* Shelled and damaged by the Japanese submarine I 17 in a position 40 N, 125 W. *6.10.1942:* Torpedoed and sunk by the Japanese submarine I 25 in a position 41.30 N, 125.22 W, off Crescent City, California, while on passage from Long Beach, California, to St. John, Oregon.

IDEFJORD in 6.1921   *Steamship Historical Society of America Inc.*

16. IDEFJORD (2) (1921-1959)
Tonnages: 4,287 gross, 2,572 net, 6,307 deadweight.
Dimensions: 365.6 x 49.8 x 26.6 feet.
Machinery: Three cylinder triple-expansion steam engine by the shipbuilders.
9.4.1921: Launched by Canadian Vickers Ltd., Montreal (Yard No. 81) for NAL. *6.1921:* Delivered. *22.4.1945:* Attacked by the German submarine U 997 in a position 69.11 N, 37.07 E while on passage to Murmansk in ballast. Abandoned, but towed to Kola Inlet for temporary repairs at Murmansk. *5.8.1945:* Sailed from Murmansk. *7.9.1945:* Arrived at Gothenburg for permanent repairs. *1959:* Sold to Ila Jernstøperi A/S (Egil Alnæs, manager), Trondheim, and renamed ILAFJORD. *1960:* Sold to Japanese shipbreakers, and *21.4.1960:* arrived at Osaka for breaking up. *25.4.1960:* Demolition commenced at Sakai.

KRISTIANIAFJORD   *F. W. Hawks collection*

17. KRISTIANIAFJORD (2) (1921-1955)
Tonnages: 6,759 gross, 4,149 net, 9,050 deadweight.
Dimensions: 421.7 x 55.8 x 26.5 feet.
Machinery: Two steam turbines, double-reduction geared to a single screw shaft, by Cammell Laird & Co. Ltd., Birkenhead.
6.1921: Completed by Napier & Miller Ltd., Old Kilpatrick, Glasgow (Yard No. 231) for NAL. *1955:* Sold to Marinos & Frangos Ltd., Nassau, and renamed AGHIOS STEFANOS. *15.2.1958:* Stranded, on fire, on Gem Reef near Sandakan, in a position 05.35 N, 119.09 E. *16.2.1958:* Fire extinguished. *20.2.1958:* Refloated, and *24.2.1958:* arrived at Sandakan for examination. *18.6.1958:* Sold by Court order for £31,505. *21.8.1958:* Arrived at Hong Kong for breaking up by Hong Kong Chiap Hua Manufactory (1947) Ltd.

TOPDALSFJORD

18. TOPDALSFJORD (1) (1921-1955)
Tonnages: 4,271 gross, 2,574 net, 6,310 deadweight.
Dimensions: 365.3 x 49.7 x 26.5 feet.
Machinery: Three cylinder triple-expansion steam engine by the shipbuilders.
5.5.1921: Launched by Canadian Vickers, Ltd., Montreal (Yard No. 82) for NAL. *7.1921:* Delivered. *9.1.1955:* Arrived at Hamburg for breaking up by Eisen und Metall K.G., Lehr & Co.

19. RANDSFJORD (1) (1921-1934)
Tonnages: 3,222 gross, 1,991 net, 5,700 deadweight.
Dimensions: 339.4 x 48.5 x 21.9 feet.
Machinery: Three cylinder triple-expansion steam engine by North Eastern Marine Engineering Co. Ltd., Sunderland.
23.4.1914: Launched by R. Thompson & Sons Ltd., Sunderland (Yard No. 284) as KONGSFOS for T. Thoresen Jr., Kristiania. *6.1914:* Delivered. *1916:* Owners became A/S Manchester (T. Thoresen Jr., manager), Kristiania. *1918:* Managers became Thor Thoresen Jr. Ltd. A/S. *1920:* Owners became Skibs-A/S Thor Thoresens Linje (Otto & Thor Thoresen A/S, managers), Oslo. *1921:* Bought by NAL and renamed RANDSFJORD. *1928:* Tonnages became 3,259 gross, 2,019 net. *1934:* Sold to Rederi-A/B Gertrud (Kristian Hansen, manager), Finland, and renamed GERTRUD. *1938:* Sold to O/Y Wipu (Antti Wihuri, manager), Finland, and renamed WILJA. *17.2.1940:* Torpedoed and

RANDSFJORD *A. Duncan*

sunk by the German submarine U 48 off Bishop Rock in a position 49.00 N, 06.33 W while on a voyage from Savannah, Georgia to Antwerp.

20. TYRIFJORD (1) (1921-1944)
Tonnages: 3,080 gross, 1,881 net, 5,500 deadweight.
Dimensions: 331.7 x 46.7 x 23.1 feet.
Machinery: Three cylinder triple-expansion steam engine by North Eastern Marine Engineering Co. Ltd., Newcastle.
Laid down as WAR DENE for The Shipping Controller, London.
6.12.1919: Launched by Wood, Skinner & Co. Ltd., Newcastle (Yard No. 215) as RAMFOS for Skibs-A/S Thor Thoresens Linje (Otto & Thor Thoresen A/S, managers), Kristiania. *5.1920:* Delivered. *1921:* Bought by NAL and renamed TYRIFJORD. *19.9.1944:* Sunk by Allied aircraft near Stavenes lighthouse, south of Florø.

TYRIFJORD *Norsk Sjøfartsmuseum*

21. FØRDEFJORD (1) (1921-1924)
Tonnages: 2,116 gross, 1,262 net, 4,000 deadweight.
Dimensions: 304.2 x 44.6 x 18.3 feet.
Machinery: Three cylinder triple-expansion steam engine by the shipbuilders.
29.1.1916: Launched by Nylands Værksted, Kristiania (Yard No. 249) as KAGGEFOS for Skandinaviske Ost-Afrika Linje (T. Thoresen Jr., manager), Kristiania. *7.1916:* Delivered. *1918:* Managers became Thor Thoresen Jr. Ltd. A/S. *1919:* Owners became Skibs A/S Thor Thoresens Linje (Otto & Thor Thoresen A/S, managers), Kristiania. *1921:* Bought by NAL and renamed FØRDEFJORD. *1924:* Sold to African & Eastern Trade Corp. Ltd., Liverpool. *1925:* Renamed ASHANTIAN. *1926:* W. Nicholl became manager. *1929:* Owners became United Africa Co. Ltd., London. *1932:* Sold to Rederi A/B Bore (G. E. Sandström, manager), Sweden, and renamed ADELE. *1934:* Sold to Hellenic Lines Ltd. (P. G. Callimanopulos, manager), Greece, and renamed HELLAS. *1955:* Sold to N. G. Nicoleris & J. A. Papazuglou (Fenton S.S. Co. Ltd., managers), Greece, and renamed MEGALOCHARI. *7.1962:* Manager became G. D. Patrikios. *1965:* Owners became N. G. Nicoleris and others (same manager), Greece. *12.2.1966:* Ran aground after suffering engine failure whilst on trials after refit at Piraeus, and received such extensive damage as to be a constructive total loss. *4.4.1966:* Wreck refloated and beached in Ambelaki Bay. *4.1969:* Broken up at Perama.

22. LANGFJORD (1921-1921)
Tonnages: 964 gross, 486 net, 1,200 deadweight.
Dimensions: 212.5 x 33.7 x 12.5 feet.
Machinery: Three cylinder triple-expansion steam engine by Plenty & Sons Ltd., Newbury.
Laid down by Ardrossan Drydock & Shipbuilding Co. Ltd., Ardrossan (Yard No. 316) as SVANFOS for Otto & Thor Thoresen, Kristiania, bought on the stocks and *12.1921:* completed for NAL. *12.1921:* Sold to Det Bergenske D/S, Bergen, and renamed NOVA. *11.1922:* Sold to Coast Lines Ltd., Liverpool, and renamed CARMARTHEN COAST. *9.11.1939:* Sunk by mine 3 miles off Seaham Harbour, while on passage from Methil to London with general cargo. Two members of her crew were lost.

TANAFJORD

23. TANAFJORD (2) (1921-1954)
Tonnages: 5,922 gross, 3,599 net, 7,714 deadweight.
Dimensions: 395.8 x 53.2 x 33.1 feet.
Machinery: Three cylinder triple-expansion steam engine by David Rowan & Co. Ltd., Glasgow.
23.3.1921: Launched by Napier & Miller Ltd., Old Kilpatrick, Glasgow (Yard No. 233) for NAL. *12.1921:* Delivered. *1950:* Tonnages became 5,930 gross,

3,649 net. *14.10.1954:* Arrived at Stavanger for scrapping by Stavanger Skipsopphugging Co.

TRONDHJEMSFJORD

24. TRONDHJEMSFJORD (2) (1922-1943)
Tonnages: 6,753 gross, 4,147 net, 9,050 deadweight.
Dimensions: 421.7 x 55.8 x 26.5 feet.
Machinery: Two steam turbines, double-reduction geared to a single shaft, by Cammell Laird & Co. Ltd., Birkenhead
4.7.1921: Launched by Napier & Miller Ltd., Old Kilpatrick, Glasgow (Yard No. 232) for NAL. *1.1922:* Delivered. *27.4.1943:* Sunk by British aircraft off Ryvingen lighthouse while on passage from Bergen to Kristiansand in ballast.

SKIENSFJORD

25. SKIENSFJORD (1) (1922-1957)
Tonnages: 5,922 gross, 3,603 net, 7,714 deadweight.
Dimensions: 395.8 x 53.2 x 25.1 feet.
Machinery: Three cylinder triple-expansion steam engine by David Rowan & Co. Ltd., Glasgow.
26.1.1922: Launched by Napier & Miller Ltd., Old Kilpatrick, Glasgow (Yard No. 234) for NAL. *3.1922:* Delivered. *3.1957:* Sold to Kam Kee Navigation Co. Ltd. (Jebshun Shipping Co. Ltd., managers), Hong Kong, and renamed SHUN HING. *7.3.1959:* Arrived at Hong Kong to be broken up by Sun Sun Enterprises.

26. GURI (1923-1946)
Tonnages: 219 gross, 127 net, 275 deadweight.
Dimensions: 96.8 x 23.6 x 8.2 feet.
Machinery: 2 cylinder 2S.C.SA oil engine by J. & C. G. Bolinders Mekaniska Verkstads A/B, Stockholm.
5.1923: Launched by Framnæs Mek. Værksted A/S, Sandefjord (Yard No. 97) for NAL (the first motor vessel ordered by NAL). *1946:* Sold to Bernt Sandøy, Molde. *1948:* Sold to A/S Inger (Jacob Kjode A/S, managers), Bergen. *1.1955:* Sold to Alf Nygård (Olav K. Vassenden, manager), Bergen. *12.1956:* Sold to Oddvar Myklebust, Bergen, and renamed ROSLAGEN. *1957:* Fitted with a new 3 cylinder 2S.C.SA Union oil engine manufactured by A/S De Forenede Motorfabrikker, Bergen. *9.1964:* Sold to Ragnvald Vadseth, Oslo. *1974:* Transferred to Jan Vadseth, Oslo. *3.1975:* Sold to Johan Mostraum, Bergen. *1977:* Fitted with a new 12 cylinder 2S.C.SA oil engine manufactured by General Motors Corp., Detroit. *4.1984:* Sank alongside the quay at Hjelmås with a full cargo of sand. Later raised and repaired. *5.1984:* Renamed TOPPFJELL. *4.1985:* Sold to Magne Farestveit, Bergen. *6.12.1990:* Condemned and deleted from the Norwegian Register.

27. MARI (1923-1923) / OSLOFJORD (1) (1923-1930)
Tonnages: 215 gross, 125 net, 275 deadweight.
Dimensions: 96.5 x 23.6 x 8.9 feet.
Machinery: 2 cylinder 2S.C.SA oil engine by J. & C. G. Bolinders Mekaniska Verkstads A/B, Stockholm.
7.1923: Completed by Framnæs Mek. Værksted A/S, Sandefjord (Yard No. 98) for NAL. *1923:* Renamed OSLOFJORD. *1930:* Sold to Einar Veim, Bergen, and renamed VESTNORGE. *1957:* Transferred to Arne Veim, Bergen, and fitted with a 4 cylinder 2S.C.SA oil engine manufactured by Klöckner-Humboldt Deutz A.G., Köln in 1951. *5.1961:* Sold to Rederibolaget Greta, Finland, and renamed GRETA. *1966:* Lengthened to 128.0 feet and tonnages became 280 gross, 146 net. *1970:* Sold to Rederi-A/B Sirnek (Nils Idman, manager), Finland. *1971:* Sold to Helge Johansson, passing later to Karl Helge Johansson, and currently registered in the ownership of Margot & Svante Johansson, Finland. *1995:* Still in service.

28. LE NORVÉGIEN (1925-1934)
Tonnages: 856 gross, 479 net, 1,200 deadweight.
Dimensions: 203.7 x 30.8 x 12.0 feet.
Machinery: Three cylinder triple-expansion steam engine by the shipbuilders.
9.1916: Completed by Stettiner Oderwerke A.G., Stettin (Yard No. 658) as FRIEDEN for Johs. Thode, Germany. *4.1918:* Sold to E.A. Mackprang, Germany. *5.1918:* Transferred to C. Mackprang Jr., Germany. *1921:* Sold to Neue Dampfer-Compagnie, Germany, and renamed ROTHENBURG. *1923:* Owning company renamed as Stettiner Dampfer Co. A.G. *1925:* Bought by

LE NORVÉGIEN *Norsk Sjøfartsmuseum*

NAL and renamed LE NORVÉGIEN. *1934:* Sold to Colonial Steamships Co. Ltd. (Rogers & Co., managers), Mauritius, and renamed CARABAO. *1956:* Sold to Jivraj's Steam Navigation Co. Ltd., Kenya. *1958:* Sold for breaking up at Mombasa. *1.1959:* Demolition commenced.

DRAMMENSFJORD *Norsk Sjøfartsmuseum*

29. DRAMMENSFJORD (2) (1925-1949)
Tonnages: 5,339 gross, 3,210 net, 8,300 deadweight.
Dimensions: 400.9 x 52.4 x 28.4 feet.
Machinery: Three cylinder triple-expansion steam engine by the shipbuilders.
6.1920: Completed by Canadian Vickers Ltd., Montreal (Yard No. 74) as TATJANA for Winge & Co.'s D/S, Kristiania, later A/S Den Norske Ruslandlinje (Winge & Co., managers). *27.2.1924:* Ran ashore on Village Island, Barclay Sound, British Columbia. *5.5.1924:* Refloated but condemned. *1924:* Sold to Canadian-American Shipping Co., Vancouver. *1925:* Bought by NAL and renamed DRAMMENSFJORD. *1949:* Sold to E. Szabados, Italy, and renamed LUCIANO. *3.9.1959:* Arrived under tow at La Spezia for scrapping by S.p.A. Cantieri Navali Santa Maria.

FORDEFJORD *Norsk Sjøfartsmuseum*

30. FØRDEFJORD (2) (1926-1937)
Tonnages: 5,242 gross, 3,264 net, 8,035 deadweight.
Dimensions: 378.8 x 50.2 x 31.7 feet.
Machinery: Two 6 cylinder 4S.C.SA oil engines by A/S Burmeister & Wain's Maskin- og Skibsbyggeri, Copenhagen, driving twin screws.
15.11.1923: Launched by Odense Staalskibsværft A/S ved A. P. Moller, Odense (Yard No. 15) as EMMA MÆRSK for D/S af 1912 A/S (A. P. Moller, manager), Denmark. *2.1924:* Delivered. *1926:* Bought by NAL and renamed FØRDEFJORD. *1.1937:* Sold to Bing & Pedersens Rederi, Oslo, and renamed RENA. *11.1939:* Owning company renamed as Skips-A/S Rena (T. Sommerfeldt & Olaf Pedersen, managers), Oslo. *2.1940:* Owners taken over by E. B. Aabys Rederi, Oslo. *1954:* Fitted with two new 4 cylinder 4S.C.SA oil engines manufactured by Maschinenfabrik Augsburg-Nürnberg A.G., Augsburg. *1.1956:* Sold to Polish Ocean Lines, Poland, and renamed SLOWACKI. *1967:* Transferred to Polish Steamship Co. *2.1974:* Sold to Chaliotata Shipping Co. Ltd., Cyprus and renamed RODANTHI A. *1976:* Sold to Kefalliniaki Charis Shipping Ltd., Greece. *2.1979:* Sold for scrapping at Piraeus.

31. FOLDENFJORD (2) (1928-1929)
Tonnages: 4,900 gross, 3,015 net, 7,300 deadweight.
Dimensions: 350.0 x 50.2 x 32.4 feet.
Machinery: Three cylinder triple-expansion steam engine by the shipbuilders.
26.2.1921: Launched by Clyde Shipbuilding & Engineering Co. Ltd., Port Glasgow (Yard No. 327) as REMUS for A/S Baja California (A.O. Lindvig, manager), Kristiania. *8.1921:* Delivered. *1928:* Bought by NAL and renamed FOLDENFJORD. *1929:* Sold to A/S Oddsø (Chr. Bolin & O. Sørensen, managers), Oslo, and renamed TIVY. *1935:* Sold to Cia. Argentina de Nav.

FOLDENFJORD *Norsk Sjøfartsmuseum*

Mihanovich Ltda., Argentina, and renamed RIOGRANDE. *1942:* Owners taken over by Cia. Argentina de Nav. Dodero S.A., Argentina. *1947:* Sold to Cia. de Nav. Riogrande S.A., Panama. *20.10.1947:* Stranded in thick fog on the North Burlings, off the coast of Portugal, while on passage from Gdansk to Spezia with coal. *21.10.1947:* Broke in two and sank.

32. LARVIKSFJORD (1930-1931)
Tonnages: 3,159 gross, 1,831 net, 5,760 deadweight.
Dimensions: 349.0 x 50.2 x 20.6 feet.
Machinery: Two 8 cylinder 4S.C.SA oil engines by the shipbuilders, driving twin screws.

LARVIKSFJORD *Norsk Sjøfartsmuseum*

24.3.1930: Launched by A/B Götaverken, Gothenburg, (Yard No. 433) for NAL. *5.1930:* Delivered. *26.9.1931:* Fire broke out in her timber cargo when near Almagrundet during a voyage from Hernösand to Montreal. Taken in tow for Stockholm by the Neptunbolaget tug HELIOS, but tug and tow ran ashore on Hovudskär in Stockholm's outer skerries. *10.1931:* Hull broke in two. *1932:* Wreck taken over by Bergnings- och Dykeri A/B Neptun, Stockholm. *24.6.1932:* Refloated and towed, with the help of floating pontoons, to Nynäshamn for survey. *1932:* Sold to A/B Götaverken, Gothenburg, for rebuilding. *5.1933:* Sold to Rederi-A/B Transatlantic (Gunnar Carlsson, manager), Sweden, and renamed KAAPAREN. *14.6.1942:* Sank after being in collision with the Norwegian m.v. TUNGSHA 3 miles off Halifax East Lightvessel while in convoy from Halifax, Nova Scotia, to the Clyde.

33. TØNSBERGFJORD (1930-1942)
Tonnages: 3,156 gross, 1,830 net, 5,750 deadweight.
Dimensions: 349.0 x 50.2 x 20.6 feet.
Machinery: Two 8 cylinder 4S.C.SA oil engines by the shipbuilders, driving twin screws.
24.3.1930: Launched by A/B Götaverken, Gothenburg (Yard No. 434) for NAL. *5.1930:* Delivered. *6.3.1942:* Torpedoed and sunk by the Italian submarine ENRICO TAZZOLI in a position 31.22 N, 68.05 W, 200 miles west of Bermuda, while on passage from Bombay to New York. One member of her crew was lost.

LYNGENFJORD   W.S.P.L.

34. LYNGENFJORD (2) (1933-1938)
Tonnages: 5,627 gross, 3,422 net, 7,615 deadweight.
Dimensions: 408.0 x 55.0 x 26.8 feet.
Machinery: Four cylinder quadruple-expansion steam engine by D. Rowan & Co., Glasgow.
7.2.1913: Launched by Wm. Hamilton & Co. Ltd., Port Glasgow (Yard No. 238) as COLUSA for New York & Pacific Steamship Co. Ltd., London. *3.1913:* Delivered. *1915:* Owners taken over by Grace Steamship Co. Inc. (W.R. Grace & Co., managers), USA. *1927:* Renamed SANTA CECELIA. *1930:* Sold to A/S Krogstads Dampskibsrederi II (Alf L. Ombustvedt, manager), Oslo, and renamed NIDAROS. *1933:* Bought by NAL and renamed LYNGENFJORD. *14.1.1938:* Went aground 15 miles west of Cape St. Francis, near Port Elizabeth, while on a voyage from Norway to Madagascar with timber and general cargo.

LE NORVÉGIEN II   A. Duncan

35. LE NORVÉGIEN II (1934-1952)
Tonnages: 1,058 gross, 605 net, 1,200 deadweight.
Dimensions: 243.7 x 34.2 x 14.1 feet.
Machinery: Three cylinder triple-expansion steam engine by Hannoversche Maschinenbau A.G., Hanover.
20.5.1921: Launched by Schiffswerft und Maschinenfabrik (vorm Janssen & Schmilinsky) A.G., Hamburg (Yard No. 576) as MINNA for Flensburger Dampfer Compagnie (H. Schuldt, manager), Germany. Her length then was 215.8 feet. *11.1921:* Delivered. *1922:* Sold to Roland Linie A.G., Germany, and renamed AMSEL. *1923:* Vessel lengthened to 243.7 feet. *1926:* Owners taken over by Norddeutscher Lloyd A.G., Germany. *1927:* Sold to Koninklijke Nederlandsche Stoomboot Maatschappij, Netherlands, and renamed PROTEUS. *1934:* Bought by NAL and renamed LE NORVÉGIEN II. *1952:* Sold to South East Asia Shipping Co. (Private) Ltd., India. *1953:* Renamed MAHAKHURSHEED. *5.1960:* Sold for breaking up at Bombay.

RANDSFJORD   W.S.S. Brownell collection

36. RANDSFJORD (2) (1937-1940)
Tonnages: 3,999 gross, 2,369 tons net, 7,465 deadweight.
Dimensions: 407.1 x 55.3 x 22.6 feet.
Machinery: Two 7 cylinder 2S.C.SA Burmeister & Wain oil engines by the shipbuilders, driving twin screws.
9.12.1936: Launched by Eriksbergs Mekaniska Verkstads A/B, Gothenburg (Yard No. 269) for NAL. *4.1937:* Delivered. *22.6.1940:* Torpedoed and sunk by the German submarine U 30 approximately 70 miles south east of Queenstown while on a voyage from New York to Liverpool, with general cargo. 4 members of her crew were lost.

KONGSFJORD *Norsk Sjøfartsmuseum*

37. KONGSFJORD (1) (1937-1940)
Tonnages: 4,000 gross, 2,365 net, 7,465 deadweight.
Dimensions: 407.1 x 55.3 x 22.6 feet.
Machinery: Two 7 cylinder 2S.C.SA Burmeister & Wain oil engines by the shipbuilders, driving twin screws.
16.4.1937: Launched by Eriksbergs Mekaniska Verkstads A/B, Gothenburg (Yard No. 270) for NAL. *7.1937:* Delivered. *17.5.1940:* Seized by the German Kriegsmarine at Oslo. *1.1941:* Refitted as a blockade runner and renamed SPERRBRECHER 15. *24.4.1941:* Renamed GONZENHEIM and fitted out as a reconnaissance ship for the battleship BISMARCK. Managed by Unterweser Reederei GmbH, Bremen. *17.5.1941:* Put to sea from a French port. *4.6.1941:* Located by aircraft from HMS VICTORIOUS and when HMS NELSON and NEPTUNE intercepted her, it was decided to scuttle and she was set on fire. She was finally torpedoed and sunk by HMS NEPTUNE.

38. OSLOFJORD (2) (1938-1940) Passenger ship
Tonnages: 18,673 gross, 10,712 net.
Dimensions: 563.5 x 73.4 x 34.1 feet.
Machinery: Four 7 cylinder 2S.C.DA oil engines by Maschinenfabrik Augsburg-Nürnberg A.G., Augsburg, driving twin screws.
Passengers: 152 Cabin Class, 307 Tourist Class, 401 3rd. Class.
29.12.1937: Launched by Deutsche Schiff-und Maschinenbau A.G. Weser, Bremen (Yard No. 932) for NAL. *5.1938:* Delivered. *1.12.1940:* Damaged by

OSLOFJORD

an acoustic mine off the River Tyne while on a voyage from Halifax, Nova Scotia, to the Tyne with mail and general cargo, and beached south of South Tyne Pier. *21-22.1.1941:* Fore end capsized and the vessel became a total loss. One member of her crew was lost.

39. VINDAFJORD (1) (1947-1951)
Tonnages: 7,263 gross, 5,249 net, 10,310 deadweight.
Dimensions: 424.6 x 57.0 x 34.9 feet.
Machinery: 3 cylinder triple-expansion steam engine by Filer & Stowell Co., Milwaukee, Wisconsin.
6.9.1943: Launched by Southeastern Shipbuilding Corp., Savannah, Georgia (Yard No. 22) as JEROME K. JONES for the United States War Shipping Administration. *9.1943:* Delivered. *1947:* Bought by NAL for operation by Skips-A/S Malmtransport and renamed VINDAFJORD. *1951:* Sold to Palmar Cia. Naviera S.A. (C. D. Pateras, manager), Liberia, and renamed GLADIATOR. *1960:* Sold to Maritenia Shipping Co. Ltd. (Pomorsko Bagersko Poduzece ''Bager'', managers), Yugoslavia, and renamed SOLTA. *1960:* Transferred to Pomorsko Bagersko Poduzece ''Bager'', Yugoslavia. *1960:* Owners became Opca Plovidba. *1963:* Sold to Jadranska Slobodna Plovidba, Yugoslavia. *1968:* Sold to Eftavrysses Cia. Naviera S.A., Cyprus, and renamed PANAGHIA KYKKOU. *18.2.1972:* Arrived at Karachi for breaking up by Younnus & Hashim Ganches.

VINDAFJORD *Norsk Sjøfartsmuseum*

FRIERFJORD *Gerhard Müller-Debus*

40. FRIERFJORD (2) (1947-1970)
Tonnages: 5,231 gross, 3,006 net, 7,960 deadweight.
Dimensions: 393.2 x 60.1 x 24.9 feet.
Machinery: Two 6 cylinder 2S.C.SA oil engines by Nordberg Manufacturing Co., Milwaukee, single reduction geared to a single shaft.
24.12.1943: Launched by Pennsylvania Shipyards Inc., Beaumont, Texas (Yard No. 293) as CAPE LOPEZ for the United States War Shipping Administration. *3.1944:* Delivered. *2.1947:* Bought by NAL and renamed FRIERFJORD. *3.1970:* Sold to Arne Teigen & Jens Hetland, Egersund, and renamed RYTTERSUND. *1972:* Sold to Chinese buyers. *10.1.1972:* Arrived at Shanghai. *14.1.1972:* Delivered to her new owners, it is believed for demolition.

RANENFJORD

41. RANENFJORD (2) (1947-1969)
Tonnages: 3,801 gross, 2,206 net, 6,390 deadweight.
Dimensions: 406.6 x 54.1 x 20.0 feet.
Machinery: 7 cylinder 2S.C.SA Götaverken oil engine by A/B Karlstads Mekaniska Verkstad, Karlstad.

14.5.1947: Launched A/B Lindholmens Varv, Gothenburg (Yard No. 995) for NAL. *10.1947:* Delivered. *30.12.1968:* Ran aground on a coral reef off Tulear, Madagascar, while on passage from Dakar to Reunion with general cargo. *10.1.1969:* Refloated and towed to Tulear. *28.1.1969:* Left Tulear for Durban, where she was condemned following survey, declared a constructive total loss and sold for £45,000 to Spanish shipbreakers. *7.3.1969:* Left Durban under tow of the German tug ALBATROS. *21.4.1969:* Arrived at Cartagena. *5.1969:* F. G. Ballester started demolition.

LYNGENFJORD

42. LYNGENFJORD (3) (1948-1970)
Tonnages: 3,800 gross, 2,201 net, 6,390 deadweight.
Dimensions: 406.6 x 54.1 x 20.0 feet.
Machinery: 7 cylinder 2S.C.SA Götaverken oil engine by A/B Karlstads Mekaniska Verkstad, Kristinehamn.
17.10.1947: Launched by A/B Lindholmens Varv, Gothenburg (Yard No. 996) for NAL. *2.1948*: Delivered. *1970:* Sold to A/S Amronto & Co. (Sverre Amundsen, manager), Haugesund, and renamed AMRONTO. *1976:* Sold to Cardigan Bay Shipping Co. Ltd. (Gulfeast Ship Management Ltd., managers), Panama, and renamed EASTERN VALOUR. *7.12.1979:* Laid up at Karachi. *17.4.1980:* Arrived at Kaohsiung for scrapping by Chi Young Steel Enterprise Co.

43. VISTAFJORD (1) (1948-1955)
Tonnages: 7,168 gross, 5,021 net, 10,310 deadweight.
Dimensions: 424.6 x 57.2 x 34.9 feet.
Machinery: 3 cylinder triple-expansion steam engine by Canadian Allis-Chalmers Ltd., Montreal.
17.7.1944: Launched by Burrard Dry Dock Co. Ltd., Vancouver (Yard No. 217) as KOOTENAY PARK for the Canadian Government (Park Steamship Co. Ltd., managers). *9.1944:* Completed as MOHAWK PARK, having been renamed while fitting out, and chartered immediately to the Ministry of War Transport, London. *1947:* Sold to Kerr-Silver Lines (Canada) Ltd., Canada, and renamed MANX SAILOR. *1948:* Bought by Skips-A/S Malmtransport (NAL, managers)

VISTAFJORD *Norsk Sjøfartsmuseum*

and renamed VISTAFJORD. *1955:* Sold to Franco Maresca fu Mariano (Mariano Maresca & Co., managers), Italy, and renamed MAR CHETO. *1963:* Transferred to Fort Steamship Co. S.A., Panama, and renamed DARING. *7.8.1966:* Arrived at La Spezia to be broken up by S.p.A. Cantieri Navali Santa Maria. *9.1966:* Work began.

OSLOFJORD *W.S.P.L. Slide collection*

44. OSLOFJORD (3) (1949-1969)/FULVIA (1969-1970) Passenger ship
Tonnages: 16,844 gross, 9,306 net.
Dimensions: 545.4 x 72.3 x 25.1 feet.
Machinery: Two 7 cylinder 2S.C.DA oil engines by Gebr. Stork & Co. N.V., Hengelo, driving twin screws.
Passengers: 266 1st. Class, 359 Tourist Class.
2.4.1949: Launched by N.V. Nederlandsche Dok en Scheepsbouw Maatschappij, Amsterdam (Yard No. 410) for NAL. *11.1949:* Delivered. *1964:*

Tonnages became 16,923 gross, 9,037 net. *6.1966:* Unsuccessful negotiations took place for sale to Finnlines Ltd. O/Y, Finland. *11.1966:* Refit started by the shipbuilders. *2.1967:* Refit completed. *12.1967-10.1968:* Operated by Greek Line, cruising from Southampton. *12.1969:* Chartered for three years to Costa Armatori S.p.A., Italy, and renamed FULVIA. *19.7.1970:*

FULVIA

An explosion in the engine room set her on fire off Teneriffe, but the passengers and crew escaped in the lifeboats. The burning ship was taken in tow for Teneriffe, but sank in a position 29.57 N, 16.30 W.

TRONDHJEMSFJORD *Norsk Sjøfartsmuseum*

45. TRONDHJEMSFJORD (3) (1950-1955)
Tonnages: 3,941 gross, 2,243 net, 7,180 deadweight.
Dimensions: 365.2 x 57.3 x 20.2 feet.
Machinery: 4 cylinder compound steam engine by the shipbuilders.
23.9.1947: Launched by A/S Fredriksstad Mekaniske Verksted, Fredrikstad (Yard No. 308) as RINGERD for Olav Ringdal, Oslo. *11.1947:* Delivered. *1949:* Owners became Ringdals Rederi A/S, Skibs A/S Ringwood & Skibs A/S Ringulv (Olav Ringdal, manager). *3.1950:* Bought by NAL and renamed

42

TRONDHJEMSFJORD. *2.1955:* Sold to Skibs-A/S Preba & Skibs-A/S Garm (Prebensen & Blakstad, managers), Risør, and renamed FOLKE BERNADOTTE. *8.1966:* Sold to Cia. de Naviera Sanblina S.A., Liberia, and renamed SPRING. *27.12.1970:* Went aground in Vasto harbour when inward bound from Antwerp. *22.5.1971:* Left Taranto in tow and *25.5.1971:* arrived at Split to be broken up by Brodospas.

KONGSFJORD *Norsk Sjøfartsmuseum*

46. KONGSFJORD (2) (1951-1972)
Tonnages: 5,934 gross, 3,408 net, 8,300 deadweight.
Dimensions: 449.7 x 57.8 x 25.7 feet.
Machinery: 5 cylinder 2S.C.SA Burmeister & Wain oil engine by J.G. Kincaid & Co. Ltd., Greenock.
30.3.1951: Launched by Lithgows Ltd., Port Glasgow, (Yard No. 1061) for NAL. *6.1951:* Delivered. *1972:* Sold to Thome & Co. (Private) Ltd., Singapore, and renamed TIMUR STAR. *1974:* Owners became Timur Nav. Private Ltd. (Thome & Co. (Private) Ltd., managers), Singapore. *1975:* Sold to Ajax Transport Corp. (Maldives Shipping Ltd., managers), Singapore, and renamed MARIYA. *24.9.1979:* Arrived at Ulsan to be scrapped by Kyung II Industry Co. Ltd.

TYRIFJORD *A. Duncan*

47. TYRIFJORD (2) (1953-1972)
Tonnages: 5,243 gross, 2,892 net, 8,100 deadweight.
Dimensions: 417.3 x 58.2 x 24.6 feet.
Machinery: 6 cylinder 2S.C.DA oil engine by Gebr. Stork & Co. N.V., Hengelo.

Laid down by A/S Bergens Mekaniske Verksteder, Bergen (Yard No. 393) for Halfdan Kuhnle, Bergen. Bought on the stocks and *5.12.1952:* launched for NAL. *14.3.1953:* Delivered. *1.1964:* Ran aground near Bec d'Ambes in the River Gironde in fog when giving way for an oncoming vessel. Refloated some days later, repaired, and re-entered service. *1972:* Sold to Jens Hetland & Arne Teigen (Arne Teigen, manager), Egersund, and renamed RYTTERSUND. *5.1976:* Sold to Arden Bay Shipping Co. Ltd. (Univan Ship Management Ltd., managers), Panama, and renamed UNITED FORTRESS. *7.8.1979:* Dragged her anchors and went aground during heavy weather in the Bay of Bengal while on voyage from Chalna to Chittagong in ballast. *9.8.1979:* Developed a severe list and was abandoned by her crew in a position 21.46 N, 90.39 E. Subsequently declared a constructive total loss.

FOLDENFJORD   Norsk Sjøfartsmuseum

48. FOLDENFJORD (3) (1953-1972)
Tonnages: 3,857 gross, 2,080 net, 6,400 deadweight.
Dimensions: 406.6 x 54.1 x 20.0 feet.
Machinery: 7 cylinder 2S.C.SA Götaverken oil engine by the shipbuilders.
15.4.1953: Launched by A/B Lindholmens Varv, Gothenburg (Yard No. 1018) for NAL. *7.1953:* Delivered. *1972:* Sold to Guan Guan Enterprising (Hong Kong) Ltd., Hong Kong, and renamed NEW OCEAN. *1972:* Transferred to the Singapore register. *1974:* Sold to Chung Chiao Shipping (Private) Ltd., Singapore. *1976:* Sin Chiao Shipping (Private) Ltd. appointed managers. *3.6.1980:* Arrived at Kaohsiung to be broken up by Nan Long Steel & Iron Co.

49. NOREFJORD (2) (1953-1972)
Tonnages: 5,246 gross, 2,887 net, 8,150 deadweight.
Dimensions: 417.3 x 58.2 x 24.6 feet.
Machinery: 8 cylinder 2S.C.SA oil engine by Sulzer Bros. Ltd., Winterthur.
15.5.1953: Launched by A/S Bergens Mekaniske Verksteder, Bergen (Yard No. 395) for NAL. *8.1953:* Delivered. *1972:* Sold to I/S Nor (A. I. Langfeldt & Co., managers), Kristiansand, and renamed ROBIN HOOD. *1973:* Sold to Argostoli Cia. Naviera S.A. (Gerasimos Kalogeratos, manager), Greece, and

NOREFJORD, 13.7.1969 　　　　　　　　　　　　　　　　　　*Joachim Pein*

renamed NISSOS ITHAKI. *24.11.1981:* Ran aground near Gizan. *13.12.1981:* Refloated, but declared a constructive total loss. *14.1.1982:* Arrived at Karachi for breaking up.

LE NORVÉGIEN III 　　　　　　　　　　　　　　　　　　*Norsk Sjøfartsmuseum*

50. LE NORVÉGIEN III (1954-1971)
Tonnages: 1,329 gross, 631 net, 1,676 deadweight.
Dimensions: 223.7 x 34.8 x 18.9 feet.
Machinery: 6 cylinder 2S.C.SA oil engine by Nydqvist & Holm A/S, Trollhättan.
24.11.1953: Launched by Norrköpings Varv och Verkstad A/B, Norrköping (Yard No. 145) for NAL. *5.2.1954:* Delivered. *1971:* Sold to Lian Soon Shipping & Trading Co. (Pte.) Ltd., Singapore. *1972:* Renamed CHERRY JAYA. *1983:* Owners' title altered to Lian Soon Shipping & Trading Co. Pte. Ltd. *1983:* Sold to Express Shipping Co. Ltd., Thailand, and renamed EXPRESS MARINE. *3.8.1984:* Badly damaged by fire when lying off Samut Prakara. *10.1984:* Sold for breaking up in the Bangkok area.

VINDAFJORD
Norsk Sjøfartsmuseum

51. VINDAFJORD (2) (1955-1964) Ore/oil bulk carrier
Tonnages: 8,844 gross, 5,223 net, 12,360 deadweight.
Dimensions: 480.9 x 59.4 x 35.8 feet.
Machinery: 7 cylinder 2S.C.SA oil engine by the shipbuilders.
17.12.1954: Launched by A/B Götaverken, Gothenburg (Yard No. 691) for Skips-A/S Malmtransport (NAL, managers). *1955:* Delivered. *1964:* Sold to Partrederiet för m.s. Ledarö (K. G. Källström, manager), Sweden, and renamed LEDARÖ. *1965:* Transferred to Rederi A/B Regnator (same manager), Sweden. *1967:* Owners taken over by Salenrederierna A/B, Sweden. *1970:* Owners now Rederi-A/B Rex, Sweden. *6.1975:* Sold to VEB Deutfracht/Seereederei, German Democratic Republic, and renamed MAXHÜTTE. *30.1.1985:* Arrived at Setubal, for breaking up by Joao Luis Russo & Filhos Ltda. *15.6.1985:* Work commenced.

DRAMMENSFJORD
Norsk Sjøfartsmuseum

52. DRAMMENSFJORD (3) (1955-1974)
Tonnages: 3,812 gross, 2,118 net. 6,400 deadweight.
Dimensions: 406.5 x 54.1 x 20.0 feet.
Machinery: 7 cylinder 2S.C.SA Götaverken oil engine by the shipbuilders.
19.1.1955: Launched by A/B Lindholmens Varv, Gothenburg (Yard No. 1032) for NAL. *4.1955:* Delivered. *1974:* Sold to Santa Filothei Cia. Naviera S.A., Greece, and renamed PISTIS. *10.1977:* Detained at Luanda, and subsequently taken over by the Angolan authorities. *1995:* Deleted from Lloyd's Register and although still entered in one of the current Greek Shipping Registers, she is believed to be no longer in existence. It seems likely that she was broken up at about the same time as her sister ELPIS (ex TANAFJORD) (No. 55)

VIGRAFJORD *Norsk Sjøfartsmuseum*

53. VIGRAFJORD (1) (1955-1960)
Tonnages: 6,145 gross, 3,658 net, 10,100 deadweight.
Dimensions: 485' 0" x 61' 0" x 26' 8"
Machinery: 5 cylinder 2S.C.SA Burmeister & Wain oil engine by J. G. Kincaid & Co. Ltd., Greenock.
4.4.1955: Launched by Short Brothers Ltd., Sunderland (Yard No. 520) for Skips-A/S Malmtransport (NAL, managers). *7.1955:* Delivered. *1960:* Sold to Ocean Tramping Co. Ltd., Hong Kong, and renamed OCEANTRAMP (registered at Glasgow). *1970:* Sold to Nan Yang Shipping Co. (Ocean Tramping Co. Ltd., Hong Kong, managers), Somalia, and renamed ORIENTAL. *26.6.1973:* Ran aground 14 miles south of Karachi in a position 24.36 N, 67.07 E, while on passage from China, and was abandoned as a constructive total loss. Wreck later sold to Taisei Kaihatsu K.K. and Nichimen K.K., Japan; refloated and sold to Taiwan for breaking up.

54. BERGENSFJORD (2) (1956-1971) Passenger ship
Tonnages: 18,739 gross, 10,047 net.
Dimensions: 578' 3" x 72' 2" x 27' 6"
Machinery: Two 8 cylinder 2S.C.DA oil engines by N.V. Gebr. Stork & Co., Hengelo, driving twin screws.
Passengers: 878.
18.7.1955: Launched by Swan, Hunter & Wigham Richardson Ltd., Wallsend-on-Tyne (Yard No. 1849) for NAL. *14.5.1956:* Delivered and registered at Bergen. *1971:* Sold to Cie. Generale Transatlantique, France, and renamed DE GRASSE. *1973:* Sale proposed to Home Lines, with charter for cruises in the Far East, for which she was to have been renamed COSTA RIVIERA. Sale did not proceed and renaming did not take place. *1973:* Sold to Thoresen

BERGENSFJORD

Norsk Sjøfartsmuseum

& Co. (Singapore) Pty. Ltd. and Bruusgaard Kiosterud & Co., Singapore, and renamed RASA SAYANG. Owners subsequently became Thoresen & Co. Ltd., Singapore, and later Thoresen & Co. (Singapore) Pte. Ltd., Singapore. *1978:* Sold to Sunlit Cruises Ltd. (M. Stroubakis, manager), Cyprus, and renamed GOLDEN MOON. *11.12.1978:* Laid up at Piraeus. *1980:* Transferred to Aphrodite Maritime Co. (M. Stroubakis, manager), Greece, and renamed RASA SAYANG. *17.8.1980:* Fire broke out in the engine room while the vessel was being refitted at Perama, and engulfed the whole ship. She was towed out of the harbour and beached near Kynosoura, where she later capsized.

TANAFJORD

Norsk Sjøfartsmuseum

55. TANAFJORD (3) (1956-1974)
Tonnages: 3,832 gross, 2,137 net, 6,450 deadweight.
Dimensions: 423' 6" x 54' 1" x 23' 4.25"
Machinery: 7 cylinder 2S.C.SA Götaverken oil engine by the shipbuilders.
27.6.1956: Launched by A/B Lindholmens Varv, Gothenburg (Yard No. 1051)

for NAL. *1.11.1956:* Delivered. *1974:* Sold to Santa Sofia Cia. Naviera S.A. (Kollintzas Marine Co. S.A., managers), Greece, and renamed ELPIS. *11.1977:* Seized at Luanda by the Angolan authorities. *24.10.1979:* Arrived at Kaohsiung to be broken up by Chi Young Steel Enterprise Co. Ltd.

Note:- PISTIS (No. 52) and ELPIS (No. 55) were the innocent victims of the Angolan Government's reaction to a major fraud concerning cargoes of ground-nuts.

LE SCANDINAVE   *Norsk Sjøfartsmuseum*

56. LE SCANDINAVE (1957-1978)
Tonnages: 1,437 gross, 732 net, 1,688 deadweight.
Dimensions: 238' 0'' x 35' 4'' x 15' 6.5''
Machinery: 7 cylinder 2S.C.SA Nohab Polar oil engine by Nydqvist & Holm A/S, Trollhättan.
27.4.1957: Launched by Drammen Slip & Verksted, Drammen (Yard No. 42), for NAL (Scandinavian East Africa Line, managers). *6.9.1957:* Delivered. *11.1978:* Sold to Ministère des Transportes du Ravitaillement et du Tourisme, Madagascar. *1979:* Renamed VATSY. *1984:* Owners became Cie. Malgache de Navigation, Madagascar. *1995:* Still in service.

SKIENSFJORD   *A. Duncan*

57. SKIENSFJORD (2) (1958-1977)
Tonnages: 3,787 gross, 2,086 net, 6,400 deadweight.
Dimensions: 423' 7'' x 54' 2'' x 23' 4.25''
Machinery: 7 cylinder 2S.C.SA Götaverken oil engine by the shipbuilders.

8.5.1958: Launched by A/B Lindholmens Varv, Gothenburg (Yard No. 1060), for NAL. *16.9.1958:* Delivered. *6.1977:* Sold to Southland Maritime Inc. (Diamantides Maritime Co., Ltd., managers), Greece, and renamed DIAMANT. *1980:* Sold to Jebel Ali National Marine, United Arab Emirates, and renamed JEBEL ALI 2. *1983:* Sold to Mohammed Khalifa Bin Salama Al Hamly, United Arab Emirates, and renamed SALAMAH-5. *1987:* Renamed AL QASIM. *10.5.1987:* Arrived at Gadani Beach for scrapping by World Marine Shipping & Trading (Pvt.) Ltd. *16.5.1987:* Work commenced.

TOPDALSFJORD as built *Norsk Sjøfartsmuseum*

58. TOPDALSFJORD (2) (1959-1978)
Tonnages: 1959-1977: 5,840 gross, 3,343 net, 7,720 deadweight.
1977 on: 5,893 gross, 2,992 net, 7,830 deadweight.
Dimensions: 423' 7'' x 54' 2'' x 26' 8.5''
Machinery: 7 cylinder 2S.C.SA Götaverken oil engine by the shipbuilders.
8.7.1959: Launched by A/B Lindholmens Varv, Gothenburg (Yard No. 1062) for NAL. *1977:* Rebuilt as a container ship by Aalborg Værft. *12.1978:* Sold to Bulakul Shipping Co. S.A. (Chin Seng Hong Ltd., Hong Kong, managers), Panama, and renamed BOONKRONG. *6.1979:* Sold to Mah Boonkrong Shipping Co. Ltd. (same managers), Thailand. *3.1981:* Sold to China Ocean Shipping Co., People's Republic of China, and renamed JIN XIAN QUAN. *1983:* Transferred to the Government of the People's Republic of China (Bureau of Maritime Transport Administration, Qingdao Branch). *1985:* Transferred to Shandong Province Marine Shipping Co., People's Republic of China. *1995:* Still in service.

TOPDALSFJORD as a container ship

VISTAFJORD   Norsk Sjøfartsmuseum

59. VISTAFJORD (2) (1960-1972) / KONGSFJORD (3) (1972-1977)
Tonnages: 9,945 gross, 5,609 net, 13,700 deadweight.
Dimensions: 501' 0" x 63' 8" x 30' 7"
Machinery: 4 cylinder 2S.C.SA Burmeister & Wain oil engine by J. G. Kincaid & Co. Ltd., Greenock.
14.10.1959: Launched by Swan, Hunter & Wigham Richardson Ltd., Wallsend-on-Tyne (Yard No. 1913) for Skips-A/S Malmtransport (NAL, managers). *2.1960:* Delivered. *1972:* Renamed KONGSFJORD, to free the name VISTAFJORD for a new cruise ship. *1973:* Transferred to NAL. *9.1977:* Sold to Navtransport Shipping Ltd., Cyprus, and renamed KAADERSHAIKH. *11.12.1982:* Arrived at Gadani Beach, for breaking up by Ilyas Investments Ltd. *4.4.1983:* Work commenced.

KONGSFJORD

IDEFJORD as a container ship

60. IDEFJORD (3) (1960-1981)
Tonnages: 1960-1977: 5,616 gross, 3,098 net, 7,875 deadweight.
           1977 on: 5,720 gross, 3,035 net, 8,139 deadweight.
Dimensions: 423' 8'' x 54' 2'' x 26' 8.5''
Machinery: 7 cylinder 2S.C.SA Götaverken oil engine by the shipbuilders.
16.2.1960: Launched by A/B Lindholmens Varv, Gothenburg (Yard No. 1063) for NAL. *1977:* Rebuilt as a container ship by Aalborg Værft. *9.1981:* Sold to Wei Chiao Shipping Pte. Ltd., Singapore, and renamed NEW PEACOCK. *3.1.1985:* Arrived at Lianyungang for breaking up by Chinese shipbreakers.

ALTAFJORD, as built, in 5.1967   *Michael Lennon*

61. ALTAFJORD (1962-1978)
Tonnages: 1962-1969: 6,299 gross, 3,953 net, 8,540 deadweight.
           1969 on: 5,995 gross, 3,746 net, 9,800 deadweight.
Dimensions: 1962-1969: 461' 5'' x 63' 2'' x 26' 5''
              1969 on: 505' 3'' x 63' 2'' x 26' 1.5''
Machinery: 6 cylinder 2S.C.SA oil engine by Sulzer Bros. Ltd., Winterthur. Ordered from A/S Bergens Mekaniske Verksteder, Bergen (Yard No. 427) by J. Ludwig Mowinckels Rederi, Bergen, bought during construction and *5.5.1962:* launched for NAL. *11.8.1962:* Delivered. *1969:* Lengthened by A/B Götaverken, Gothenburg. *1.4.1969:* During reconstruction, the forepart heeled over and sank, but was righted *18.4.1969*. *6.1978:* Sold to A. Bottacchi S.A. de Navegacion, Argentina, and renamed PUNTA NORTE. *1985:* Renamed NORTE. *18.1.1986:* Arrived at Porto Alegre, Brazil, for breaking up by Estaleiro So S.A. *4.2.1986:* Work began.

ALTAFJORD after being lengthened *Norsk Sjøfartsmuseum*

VIGRAFJORD

62. VIGRAFJORD (2) (1963-1975)
Tonnages: 1963-1970: 6,301 gross, 3,976 net, 8,540 deadweight.
             1970 on: 6,017 gross, 3,778 net, 9,800 deadweight.
Dimensions: 1963-1970: 461' 6" x 63' 3" x 26' 5"
              1970 on: 504' 7" x 63' 2" x 26' 1.5"
Machinery: 6 cylinder 2S.C.SA oil engine by Sulzer Bros. Ltd., Winterhur.
28.2.1963: Launched by Drammen Slip & Verksted, Drammen (Yard No. 53) for NAL. *6.1963:* Delivered. *1970:* Lengthened by A/B Götaverken, Gothenburg. *6.1975:* Sold to P. N. Djäkarta Lloyd, Indonesia, and renamed DJATIWANGI. *1980:* Owners became Jakarta Lloyd P. T. Perusahaan Pelayaran Samudra, Indonesia. *24.4.1983:* Arrived at Alang, for breaking up by Indian Metal Traders.

63. VIKSFJORD (1964-1968)
Tonnages: 5,163 gross, 2,760 net, 7,900 deadweight.
Dimensions: 412' 4" x 60' 2" x 24' 9.75"
Machinery: Two 6 cylinder 2S.C.SA oil engines by Nordberg Manufacturing Co., Milwaukee, single-reduction geared to a single shaft.
23.4.1944: Launched by Pennsylvania Shipyards Inc., Beaumont, Texas (Yard No. 299) as CAPE GASPE for the United States War Shipping Administration (operated by Grace Line Inc.). *6.1944:* Completed. *16.10.1947:* Sold to Rederiet Ocean A/S (Rederiet J. Lauritzen, managers), Denmark, and renamed GERDA

VIKSFJORD

DAN. *23.5.1961:* Sold to Wilh. Wilhelmsen, Tønsberg, and renamed TYSLA. *11.5.1964:* Bought by NAL, and renamed VIKSFJORD. *6.1968:* Sold to Jens Hetland, Egersund, and renamed RYTTERVIK. *10.1.1972:* Arrived at Shanghai for breaking up by China National Machinery Import & Export Corp.

64. SUNNDALSFJORD (1964-1973)
Tonnages: 4,621 gross, 2,520 net, 7,300 deadweight.
Dimensions: 433' 5" x 56' 7" x 25' 0"
Machinery: 7 cylinder 2S.C.SA Götaverken oil engine by the shipbuilders.
18.2.1955: Launched by Uddevallavarvet A/B, Uddevalla (Yard No. 143) as

SUNNDALSFJORD

BOW PLATE for Skibs-A/S Hassel (A/S Rederiet Odfjell, managers), Bergen. *1964:* Bought by NAL and renamed SUNNDALSFJORD. *1973:* Sold to Bruusgaard Kiøsteruds S/A (Bruusgaard Kiøsterud & Co., managers), Drammen, and renamed HERMELIN. *1977:* Management transferred to Thoresen International, Asker. *10.1979:* Sold to Cia. Naviera Arafura S.A. (Full Wind Navigation Co. Ltd., Hong Kong, managers), Panama, and renamed ARAFURA STAR. *1980:* Renamed FULLWIND LUCKY. *6.8.1980:* Arrived at Kaohsiung for breaking up by E. Chang Iron Steel Works Co. Ltd.

SAGAFJORD as built

65. SAGAFJORD (1965-1983) Passenger ship
Tonnages: 1964-1982: 24,002 gross, 13,340 net.
          1982 on: 24,108 gross, 13,820 net.
Dimensions: 619' 8" x 80' 3" x 27' 1"
Machinery: Two 9 cylinder Sulzer oil engines by Forges et Chantiers de la Mediterranée, Le Havre, driving twin screws.
Passengers: 830
13.6.1964: Launched by Forges et Chantiers de la Mediterranée, La Seyne (Yard No. 1366) for P/R Sagafjord (NAL, managers). *1.4.1965:* Due for delivery, but heavy losses forced builders into liquidation. *2.10.1965:* Maiden voyage commenced. *1980:* Transferred to K/S Norwegian America Cruises A/S (Leif Høegh & Co. A/S, managers). *1980:* Extensively refitted by Blohm & Voss,

SAGAFJORD after reconstruction in 1980   *A. Duncan*

Hamburg. *1983:* Owners re-styled K/S Norwegian America Line Cruises A/S (same managers). *1983:* Sold to Cunard Line Ltd., registered in the Bahamas. *1993:* Transferred to The Cunard Steam-Ship Co. p.l.c. (Cunard Line Ltd., managers). *1995:* Still in service.

TAVARATRA *Norsk Sjøfartsmuseum*

66. TAVARATRA (1968-1978)
Tonnages: 496 gross, 310 net, 985 deadweight.
Dimensions: 245' 7" x 35' 7" x 11' 7.75"
Machinery: 6 cylinder 4S.C.SA oil engine by MaK Maschinenbau Kiel A.G., Kiel.
9.3.1963: Launched by Cia. Euskalduna, Bilbao (Yard No. 134) as KONG ALF for Det Søndenfjelds-Norske D/S, Oslo. *1968:* Bought by NAL and renamed TAVARATRA. *10.1978:* Sold to Potential Shipping Co., Panama. *1979:* Transferred to Fabula Shipping Co. Ltd., Cyprus, and renamed KYRIA. *1983:* Sold to Veronia Marine Ltd., Cyprus, and renamed KONTER. *1985:* Sold to Agnes Navigation Ltd., Cyprus, and renamed AUDREY. *1985:* Sold to State Trading Organisation, Maldive Islands, and renamed DHONAKULHI. Later transferred to Maldives Industrial Fisheries Co. Ltd., Maldive Islands. *1995:* Still in service.

VINDAFJORD

67. VINDAFJORD (3) (1968-1978)
Tonnages: 8,742 gross, 4,907 net, 12,540 deadweight.
Dimensions: 467' 2" x 61' 0" x 29' 8.5"
Machinery: 7 cylinder 2S.C.SA Götaverken oil engine by the shipbuilders.
28.4.1959: Launched by Uddevallavarvet A/B, Uddevalla, Sweden (Yard No. 174) as THORSCARRIER for A/S Ørnen & A/S Odd (A/S Thor Dahl, managers), Sandefjord. *1968:* Bought by Skips-A/S Malmtransport (NAL, managers), and renamed VINDAFJORD. *1972:* Transferred to NAL. *10.1978:* Sold to Frijoles Cia. Naviera S.A. (Diana Shipping Agencies S.A., managers), Greece, and renamed NORDAVE. *21.6.1979:* Ran ashore in a position 24.14 N, 67.16 E while on passage from Karachi to Kandla in ballast. Declared to be a constructive total loss. *1980:* Wreck sold to Pakistan buyers for breaking up.

RANENFJORD, 7.11.1977 *Joachim Pein*

68. RANENFJORD (3) (1971-1981)
Tonnages: 6,465 gross, 3,434 net, 11,918 deadweight.
Dimensions: 138.21 (145.70) x 22.05 x 12.37 metres. 8.014 draft.
Machinery: 7 cylinder 2S.C.SA Burmeister & Wain oil engine by Mitsui Zosen K.K., Tamano.
5.6.1971: Launched by Mitsui Zosen K.K., Osaka (Yard No. 893) for NAL. *16.9.1971:* Delivered. *9.1981:* Sold to Haewoo Shipping Co. Ltd., South Korea, and renamed HAE WOO No. 3. *1985:* Sold to Daeyang Shipping Corp. Ltd., South Korea. *1986:* Sold to Pan Ocean Shipping Co. Ltd., South Korea. *1995:* Still in service.

LYNGENFJORD

69. LYNGENFJORD (4) (1971-1981)
Tonnages: 6,467 gross, 3,434 net, 11,884 deadweight.
Dimensions: 137.98 (145.70) x 22.05 x 12.37 metres. 7.887 draft.
Machinery: 7 cylinder 2S.C.SA Burmeister & Wain oil engine by Mitsui Zosen K.K., Tamano.
12.8.1971: Launched by Mitsui Zosen K.K., Osaka (Yard No. 894) for NAL. *5.11.1971:* Delivered. *9.1981:* Sold to Haewoo Shipping Co. Ltd., South Korea, and renamed HAE WOO No. 2. *1985:* Sold to Daeyang Shipping Corp. Ltd., South Korea. *1986:* Sold to Pan Ocean Shipping Co. Ltd., South Korea. *1995:* Still in service.

VISTAFJORD, 28.7.1973   *Joachim Pein*

70. VISTAFJORD (3) (1973-1984) Passenger ship
Tonnages: 24,292 gross, 12,771 net.
Dimensions: 167.67 (191.09) x 25.05 x 16.77 metres. 8.230 draft.
Machinery: Two 9 cylinder 2S.C.SA Sulzer oil engines by G. Clark & N.E.M. Ltd., Wallsend-on-Tyne, driving twin screws.
Passengers: 635.
15.5.1972: Launched by Swan Hunter Shipbuilders Ltd., Wallsend-on-Tyne (Yard No. 39) for Sameiet Vistafjord (NAL, managers). *15.5.1973:* Delivered. *1.1.1981:* Transferred to K/S Norwegian America Cruises A/S (Leif Høegh & Co. A/S, managers). *1983:* Owners re-styled K/S Norwegian America Line Cruises A/S (same managers). *1984:* Sold to Cunard Line Ltd., registered in the Bahamas. *1993:* Transferred to The Cunard Steam-Ship Co. p.l.c. (Cunard Line Ltd., managers). *1995:* Still in service.

71. TANAFJORD (4) (1976-1981)
Tonnages: 7,365 gross, 4,481 net, 9,412 deadweight.
Dimensions: 127.49 (137.24) x 19.87 x 10.32 metres. 8.002 draft.
Machinery: 5 cylinder 2S.C.SA Sulzer oil engine by Ishikawajima-Harima Heavy Industries Co. Ltd., Aioi.
24.8.1976: Launched by Fukuoka Zosen, Fukuoka (Yard No. 1050) for NAL. *14.12.1976:* Delivered. *10.1981:* Sold to P. T. Perusahaan Pelayaran Samudera—Karana Line, Indonesia, and renamed AMBALIKA. *1995:* Still in service.

TANAFJORD, 25.10.1980　　　　　　　　　　　　　　　　　　　　　　Joachim Pein

72. OSLOFJORD (4) (1977-1981)
Tonnages: 8,060 gross, 4,977 net, 10,272 deadweight.
Dimensions: 133.56 (144.00) x 19.89 x 10.32 metres. 8.220 draft.
Machinery: 5 cylinder 2S.C.SA Sulzer oil engine by Ishikawajima-Harima Heavy Industries Co. Ltd., Aioi.
6.11.1976: Launched by Fukuoka Zosen, Fukuoka (Yard No. 1051) for NAL. *8.3.1977:* Delivered. *8.1981:* Sold to Oslofjord Inc., Liberia, and renamed AMBIKA. *3.1982:* Sold to Violet Venus Co. S.A. (P. T. Perusahaan Pelayaran Samudera—Karana Line, Indonesia, managers), Panama. *1989:* Renamed AMARANTH I. *1989:* Sold to Sea Fighter Maritime S.A., Panama, and renamed SELENE. *1991:* Sold to Everett-Orient Line Inc., Liberia, and renamed ADELFAEVERETT. *1992:* Sold to Z-River Shipping Corp., Panama, and renamed TIGER SPRING. *1994:* Zhejiang Fuchzien Shipping & Enterprises Co. Ltd. became managers. *1995:* Still in service.

OSLOFJORD, 10.5.1981　　　　　　　　　　　　　　　　　　　　　　Joachim Pein

BERGENSFJORD

73. BERGENSFJORD (3) (1977-1981)
Tonnages:- 8,060 gross, 4,976 net, 10,261 deadweight.
Dimensions: 133.56 (144.00) x 19.87 x 10.32 metres. 8.002 draft.
Machinery: 5 cylinder 2S.C.SA Sulzer oil engine by Ishikawajima-Harima Heavy Industries Co. Ltd., Aioi.
22.1.1977: Launched by Fukuoka Zosen, Fukuoka (Yard No. 1052) for NAL. *28.4.1977:* Delivered. *7.1981:* Sold to Bergensfjord Inc., Liberia, and renamed ARIMBI. *3.1982:* Sold to Violet Venus S.A. (P. T. Perusahaan Pelayaran Samudera—Karana Line, Indonesia, managers), Panama. *1989:* Renamed LATONA I. *1989:* Resold and renamed IRIS. *1991:* Sold to Everett-Orient Line Inc., Liberia, and renamed ROSALEVERETT. *1992:* Sold to Cimarron Ltd. (Pictan Shipping Agency Ltd., managers), Liberia, and renamed KING YEE. *1992:* Sold to Z-River Shipping Corp., Panama, and renamed DRAGON WELL. *1994:* Zhejiang Fuchzien Shipping & Enterprises Co. Ltd. became managers. *1995:* Still in service.

74. OSLOFJORD (5) (1984-1985) Chemical tanker
Tonnages: 16,820 gross, 11,572 net, 29,954 deadweight.
Dimensions: 162.01 (174.02) x 25.43 x 14.36 metres. 10.683 draft.
Machinery: 6 cylinder 2S.C.SA Burmeister & Wain oil engine by Mitsui Engineering & Shipbuilding Co. Ltd., Tamano.
3.3.1984: Launched by Usuki Tekkosho K.K., Saiki (Yard No. 1317) for Providential Carrier Inc., Liberia. *31.7.1984:* Completed, and bareboat chartered to K/S NAL Bulk Shipping A/S (NAL, managers), with purchase option. *1985:* Charter, completed. *1990:* Sold to Anette Tankers Inc. (Arne Blystad A/S, managers), Liberia, and renamed ANETTE. *1991:* Sold to Allegre Shipping Corp. (Maritime Overseas Corp., managers), Liberia, and renamed ALLEGRE. *1995:* Still in service.

75. BERGENSFJORD (4) (1984-1985) Chemical tanker
Tonnages: 16,820 gross, 11,572 net, 29,992 deadweight.
Dimensions: 162.01 (170.72) x 25.43 x 14.36 metres. 10.691 draft.
Machinery: 6 cylinder 2S.C.SA Sulzer oil engine by Mitsubishi Heavy Industries Ltd., Kobe.
1.3.1984: Launched by Minami-Nippon Zosen K.K., Usuki (Yard No. 565) for Providential Champion Inc., Liberia. *25.9.1984:* Completed, and bareboat chartered to K/S NAL Bulk Shipping A/S (NAL, managers), with purchase option. *1985:* Charter completed. *1988:* Sold to Paulina Transport Ltd. (OMI Corp., managers), Bahamas, and renamed PAULINA. *1989:* Sold to Saugatuck Shipping Ltd. (same managers), Liberia. *1993:* Managers became Omi Bulk Management Co. *1995:* Still in service.

STOLT VINCITA, 5.1.1989   R. Oberhem

76. STOLT VINCITA (1985-1989) Chemical tanker
Tonnages: 16,867 gross, 11,851 net, 30,899 deadweight.
Dimensions: 162.62 (170.72) x 29.55 x 13.26 metres. 9.799 draft.
Machinery: 7 cylinder 2S.C.SA Burmeister & Wain oil engine by Nylands Verksted A/S, Oslo.
1977: Built in two sections by Ankerlokken Verft Forde A/S, Forde (Yard No. 9) as VINCITA for Halfdan Ditlev-Simonsen & Co., Oslo. *5.2.1977:* Aft section launched. *26.5.1977:* Fore section launched. *10.1977:* Delivered. *1980:* Sold to K/S Siem-Vee-Ship A/S (Halfdan Ditlev-Simonsen & Co., managers), Oslo. *1984:* Sold to K/S A/S Chem Invest (Oslo Ship Management A/S, managers), Oslo, and renamed STOLT VINCITA. *1985:* Bought by Chem-Invest Inc. (Norwegian Ship Management A/S, managers), Liberia. NAL owned 26% of the vessel. *1989:* Sold to Stolt Vincita Inc. (Stolt-Nielsens Rederi A/S, managers), Liberia, and renamed STOLT VICTOR. *1990:* Owners became Stolt Victor Inc., Liberia (same managers). *1995:* Still in service.

STOLT VENTURA   W.S.P.L.

77. STOLT VENTURA (1985-1989) Chemical tanker
Tonnages: 16,866 gross, 11,851 net, 30,892 deadweight.
Dimensions: 162.57 (170.77) x 29.55 x 13.26 metres. 10.116 draft.
Machinery: 7 cylinder 2S.C.SA Burmeister & Wain oil engine by Nylands Verksted A/S, Oslo.
1977: Built in two sections by Ankerlokken Verft Forde A/S, Forde (Yard No. 10) as VENTURA for P/R Vee Ship (Halfdan Ditlev-Simonsen & Co., managers), Oslo. *11.1977:* Fore section launched. *3.2.1978:* Aft section launched. *14.6.1978:* Delivered. *1980:* Sold to K/S Siem-Vee-Ship A/S (Halfdan Ditlev-Simonsen & Co., managers), Oslo. *1985:* Bought by Chem-Invest Inc. (Norwegian Ship Management A/S, managers), Liberia, and

renamed STOLT VENTURA. NAL owned 26% of the vessel. *1989:* Sold to Stolt Ventura Inc. (Stolt-Nielsens Rederi A/S, managers), Liberia, and renamed STOLT VIKING. *1990:* Owners became Stolt Viking Inc., Liberia (same managers). *1995:* Still in service.

VIRA GAS   W.S.S. Brownell collection

78. VIRA GAS (1985-1987) Liquefied Petroleum Gas carrier
Tonnages: 9,376 gross, 4,712 net, 11,420 deadweight.
Dimensions: 127.44 (138.72) x 20.53 x 11.51 metres. 9.202 draft.
Machinery: 6 cylinder 2S.C.SA oil engine by Sulzer Brothers Ltd., Winterthur. *3.2.1976:* Launched by Moss Rosenberg Værft A/S, Moss (Yard No. 183) as FERNBANK for P/R Fernbank (Fearnley & Eger, managers), Oslo. *19.5.1976:* Delivered. *1977:* Sold to Helge R. Myhre, Stavanger, and renamed HELIOS. *1979:* Transferred to K/S A/S Helios (Helge R. Myhre, manager), Stavanger. *1982:* Managers became Rederiet Helge R. Myhre A/S. *1984:* Sold to K/S Gass-Transport A/S (A/S Sigurd Sverdrup, managers), Oslo, and renamed VIRA GAS. *1984:* Managers became Oslo Ship Management A/S. *1985:* Managers became Norwegian Ship Management A/S. NAL owned 62% of the vessel. *1987:* Sold to Seafalcon B.V. (Holland Ship Management B.V., managers), Netherlands. *1987:* Sold to K/S Nordgas (A/S Havtor Management, managers), Oslo, and placed on the Norwegian International Register. *1992:* Managers became Hydroship A/S. *1994:* Sold to P/R Clipper Victoria (Skibs-A/S Solvang, managers), Stavanger and renamed CLIPPER VICTORIA. *1995:* Still in service.

NOSAC MASCOT, 24.10.1986   Hans W. Tiedemann

79. NOSAC MASCOT (1986-1988) / NOSAC RANGER (1988-   ) Car/truck carrier
Tonnages: 16,568 gross, 9,710 net, 17,406 deadweight.
Dimensions: 180.02 (194.52) x 32.03 x 30.71 metres. 9.716 draft.

NOSAC RANGER, 29.8.1993 — *Hans W. Tiedemann*

Machinery: 6 cylinder 2S.C.SA Burmeister & Wain oil engine by the shipbuilders.
Capacity: 5,830 cars.
4.8.1978: Launched by Mitsui Engineering & Shipbuilding Co. Ltd., Tamano (Yard No. 1078) as NOPAL MASCOT for R/A Mascot (Arth. H. Mathiesen, manager), Oslo. *21.11.1978:* Delivered. *1983:* Sold to K/S Mascot Auto Transport A/S (same manager). *1983:* Transferred to Rederi A/S Mascot (same manager). *1984:* Renamed NOSAC MASCOT. *1.11.1986:* Bought by NAL (Norwegian Ship Management A/S, managers), Liberia. *7.1988:* Transferred to Carship Inc. (same managers), USA, and renamed NOSAC RANGER. *1989:* Transferred to Ranger Shipholding Corp. (Pacific Gulf Marine Inc., managers), USA. *1990:* Managers became NAL. *27.12.1990:* Transferred to Car Carrier Inc., USA (same managers). *1994:* Tonnage remeasured—47,089 gross, 15,586 net. *1995:* In the present fleet.

NOSAC BARBRO, 20.6.1989 — *Hans W. Tiedemann*

80. NOSAC BARBRO (1986-1989) / NOSAC ROVER (1989-   ) Car/truck carrier

Tonnages: 19,089 gross, 11,123 net, 10,480 deadweight.
Dimensions: 180.02 (194.49) x 32.21 x 19.87 metres. 9.719 draft.
Machinery: 6 cylinder 2S.C.SA Burmeister & Wain oil engine by the shipbuilders.
Capacity: 5,600 cars.
22.9.1982: Launched by Mitsui Engineering & Shipbuilding Co. Ltd., Tamano (Yard No. 1245) as NOPAL BARBRO for K/S Mascot Auto Transport A/S (Arth. H. Mathiesen, manager), Oslo. *20.12.1982:* Delivered. *1984:* Renamed NOSAC

NOSAC ROVER, 1.5.1995 *Hans W. Tiedemann*

BARBRO. *1986:* Bought by Nalto Inc. (Norwegian Ship Management A/S, managers), Liberia. *15.10.1988:* Transferred to Nal II Inc., Liberia (same managers). *16.10.1989:* Renamed NOSAC ROVER. *1990:* Re-registered at Oslo (NAL, managers), and placed on the Norwegian International Register. *1994:* Tonnage remeasured—47,947 gross, 15,583 net. *1995:* In the present fleet.

NOSAC SEL, 5.9.1988 *Michael Lennon*

81. NOSAC SEL (1987-1988) / OCEAN SEL (1988-1995) / SEA TRANSIT (1995-   ) Car carrier
Tonnages: 7,494 gross, 3,719 net, 10,379 deadweight.
Dimensions: 173.79 (187.51) x 22.94 x 16.79 metres. 8.006 draft.
Machinery: 8 cylinder 2S.C.SA Sulzer oil engine by Koninklijke Maatschappij 'De Schelde', Flushing.
Capacity: 3,150 cars.
18.12.1975: Launched by B.V. Machinefabriek en Scheepswerf van P. Smit Jr., Rotterdam (Yard No. 671) as NOPAL SEL for K/S Benargus A/S & Co. (Øivind Lorentzen, manager), Oslo. *30.6.1976:* Delivered. *1979:* Managers restyled Øivind Lorentzen A/S. *1984:* Renamed NOSAC SEL and transferred to Benargus Shipping Inc., Liberia (same managers). *1985:* Transferred to

OCEAN SEL in 4.1991   *Michael Cassar*

Ocean Sel S. en C. (Oslo Ship Management A/S, managers), Panama. *1985:* Bought by Ocean Car Carriers Ltd. (Norwegian Ship Management A/S, managers), Panama. *7.1987:* NAL took over 25% ownership of the vessel in conjunction with the amalgamation with Øivind Lortentzen A/S. *1988:* Renamed OCEAN SEL. *1992:* Managers became Barber Ship Management Ltd. *1.1995:* Bought by K/S Sea Transit, Oslo, of which NAL and Wilh. Wilhelmsen each own 50%, and renamed SEA TRANSIT. *1995:* Tonnage remeasured - 25,884 gross, 8,442 net. *1995:* In the present fleet.

NOSAC EXPRESS, 7.6.1988

82. NOSAC EXPRESS (1987-   ) Car/truck carrier
Tonnages: 48,357 gross, 16,723 net, 21,900 deadweight.
Dimensions: 182.40 (195.02) x 32.26 x 21.70 metres. 11.058 draft.
Machinery: 6 cylinder 2S.C.SA Burmeister & Wain oil engine by Hyundai Shipbuilding & Heavy Industries Ltd., Ulsan.
Capacity: 5,535 cars.
30.9.1984: Launched by Daewoo Shipbuilding & Heavy Machinery Ltd., Koje. (Yard No. 4402) for K/S Benargus A/S & Co. (Øivind Lorentzen Shipping A/S, managers), Oslo. *1986:* Managers became Norwegian Ship Management A/S. *7.1987:* K/S Benargus A/S & Co. taken over by NAL. *1987:* Registration transferred to Panama. *12.10.1989:* Bought by K/S Nosac Express (Norwegian Ship Management A/S, managers), re-registered at Oslo and placed on the Norwegian International Register. *1990:* Managers became NAL. *1992:*

Transferred to K/S Benargus A/S & Co., Oslo (same managers). *1995:* In the present fleet.

NOSAC BRANCO as NOPAL BRANCO, 26.6.1979   *W.S.P.L.*

83. NOSAC BRANCO (1987-1987) Car/truck carrier
Tonnages: 14,202 gross, 8,544 net.
Dimensions: 179.58 (190.58) x 22.99 x 13.31 metres. 9.919 draft.
Machinery: 6 cylinder 2S.C.SA oil engine by Sulzer Brothers Ltd., Winterthur.
Capacity: 3,670 cars.
30.11.1970: Launched by Stocznia Gdanska, Gdansk (Yard No. 444/03), as general cargo ship AMALIA (10,192 tons gross, 5,790 tons net, 150.02 x 22.99 x 13.31 metres) for Cia. de Navegacao Maritima Netumar, Brazil.
5.1971: Delivered. *1973:* Sold to Norship 73 Inc., (Øivind Lorentzen, manager) Liberia, and renamed NOPAL BRANCO. *1975:* Transferred to Partrederi Nopal Branco (Bedriftskonsulenter A/S, managers), Oslo, lengthened and rebuilt as a car carrier. *1979:* Managers restyled Øivind Lorentzen A/S. *1980:* Sold to K/S Benargus A/S & Co., Oslo (same managers). *1982:* Sold to Brancaster Shipping Inc., Liberia (same managers). *1984:* Renamed NOSAC BRANCO. Managers restyled Øivind Lorentzen Shipping A/S. *1986:* Managers became Norwegian Ship Management A/S. *7.1987:* Taken over by NAL in conjunction with the amalgamation with Øivind Lorentzen A/S. *8.1987:* Transferred to Brancaster Shipping A/S, Oslo and resold to Kuo Dar Steel Enterprise, Taiwan, for breaking up. *12.9.1987:* Arrived at Kaohsiung. *17.10.1987:* Work commenced.

84. NOSAC VERDE (1987-1987) Car/truck carrier
Tonnages: 14,202 gross, 8,649 net, 10,398 deadweight.
Dimensions: 179.58 (190.58) x 22.99 x 13.31 metres. 9.926 draft.
Machinery: 6 cylinder 2S.C.SA Burmeister & Wain oil engine by H. Cegielski, Poznan.
Capacity: 3,700 cars.
12.8.1972: Launched by Stocznia Gdanska, Gdansk (Yard No. 444/09), as general cargo ship JOANA (10,416 tons gross, 5,776 tons net, 150.02 x 22.99 x 13.31 metres) for Cia. de Navegacao Maritima Netumar, Brazil.
14.12.1972: Delivered. *1973:* Sold to Benverde 73 Inc. (Øivind Lorentzen, manager), Liberia, and renamed NOPAL VERDE. *1975:* Sold to K/S Benargus A/S & Co., Oslo (same manager), lengthened, and rebuilt as a car carrier. *1979:* Managers restyled Øivind Lorentzen A/S. *1983:* Sold to Brancaster Shipping Inc., Liberia (same managers). *1984:* Renamed NOSAC VERDE, and managers restyled Øivind Lorentzen Shipping A/S. *1986:* Managers became

NOSAC VERDE as NOPAL VERDE *W.S.P.L. Slide collection*

Norwegian Ship Management A/S. *7.1987:* Taken over by NAL in conjunction with the amalgamation with Øivind Lorentzen A/S. *9.1987:* Transferred to Brancaster Shipping A/S, Oslo and resold to King Tung Chan Enterprise, Taiwan, for breaking up. *13.9.1987:* Arrived at Kaohsiung. *26.10.1970:* Work commenced.

NOSAC STAR on trials

85. NOSAC STAR (1987-   ) Car/truck carrier
Tonnages: 49,792 gross, 15,050 net, 15,536 deadweight.
Dimensions: 180.02 (190.00) x 32.24 x 13.92 metres. 9.121 draft.
Machinery: 6 cylinder 2S.C.SA Burmeister & Wain oil engine by Mitsui Engineering & Shipbuilding Co. Ltd., Tamano.
Capacity: 5,936 cars.
31.1.1987: Launched by Tsuneishi Zosen K.K., Numakuma (Yard No. 588) for Tsusac S.A., Panama. *27.4.1987:* Delivered, and immediately bareboat chartered to K/S Benargus A/S & Co. (Norwegian Ship Management A/S, managers). *7.1987:* Ownership of K/S Benargus A/S & Co. taken over by NAL. *1990:* Bought by KS Nosac Star (NAL, managers), registered at Oslo and placed on the Norwegian International Register. *1995:* In the present fleet.

NOSAC SUN

86. NOSAC SUN (1987-) Car/truck carrier
Tonnages: 49,792 gross, 15,050 net, 15,543 deadweight.
Dimensions: 180.02 (190.00) x 32.24 x 13.92 metres. 9.121 draft.
Machinery: 6 cylinder 2S.C.SA Burmeister & Wain oil engine by Mitsui Engineering & Shipbuilding Co. Ltd., Tamano.
Capacity: 5,936 cars.
3.3.1987: Launched by Tsuneishi Zosen K.K., Numakuma (Yard No. 589) for Aisac Management S.A., Panama. *10.6.1987:* Delivered, and immediately bareboat chartered to K/S Benargus A/S & Co. (Norwegian Ship Management A/S, managers). *7.1987:* Ownership of K/S Benargus A/S & Co. taken over by NAL. *1990:* NAL became managers. *2.1994:* Bought by K/S Benargus A/S & Co. (same managers), registered at Oslo and placed on the Norwegian International Register. *1995:* In the present fleet.

NOSAC SKY

87. NOSAC SKY (1987-) Car/truck carrier
Tonnages: 49,750 gross, 15,029 net, 15,528 deadweight.
Dimensions: 180.02 (190.00) x 32.24 x 13.92 metres. 9.121 draft.
Machinery: 6 cylinder 2S.C.SA Burmeister & Wain oil engine by Mitsui Engineering & Shipbuilding Co. Ltd., Tamano.
Capacity: 5,915 cars.

1.7.1987: Launched by Tsuneishi Zosen K.K., Numakuma (Yard No. 593) for Hirosac S.A., Panama. *25.9.1987:* Delivered, and immediately bareboat chartered to K/S Benargus A/S & Co. (an NAL subsidiary) (Norwegian Ship Management A/S, managers). *1990:* Bought by K/S Benargus A/S & Co. (NAL, managers), registered at Oslo and placed on the Norwegian International Register. *1995:* In the present fleet.

NOSAC EXPLORER, 15.5.1993 — *Hans W. Tiedemann*

88. NOSAC TASCO (1988-1989) / NOSAC EXPLORER (1989-   ) Car/truck carrier

Tonnages: 48,393 gross, 16,723 net, 22,067 deadweight.
Dimensions: 182.40 (195.03) x 32.29 x 30.97 metres. 11.058 draft.
Machinery: 6 cylinder 2S.C.SA Burmeister & Wain oil engine by Hyundai Shipbuilding & Heavy Industries Ltd., Ulsan.
Capacity: 5,535 cars.
30.9.1984: Launched by Daewoo Shipbuilding & Heavy Machinery Ltd., Koje (Yard No. 4401) as NOSAC TASCO for Wilh. Wilhelmsen Ltd. A/S, Tønsberg. *7.2.1985:* Delivered. *16.1.1987:* Transferred to Panama registry. *30.12.1988:* Bought by NAL and transferred to K/S A/S Fernboat (NAL, managers), Oslo, and placed on the Norwegian International Register. *20.12.1989:* Sold to Hafslund Transport A/S, Oslo (same managers) and renamed NOSAC EXPLORER. *3.9.1992:* Sold to K/S Benargus A/S & Co., Oslo (same managers). *1995:* In the present fleet.

TARGET, 7.2.1987 — *J. McFaul collection*

89. TARGET (1988-1990) / ARMACUP PATRICIA (1990-   ) Car carrier

Tonnages: 7,274 gross, 3,626 net, 10,750 deadweight.
Dimensions: 173.67 (187.51) x 23.02 x 16.82 metres. 8.008 draft.
Machinery: 8 cylinder 2S.C.SA Sulzer oil engine by the shipbuilders.
Capacity: 3,800 cars.

27.4.1974: Launched by N.V. Koninklijke Maatschappij 'De Schelde', Flushing (Yard No. 348) as DYVI ADRIATIC for Jan-Erik Dyvi, Oslo. *16.9.1974:* Delivered. *1975:* Sold to A/S Atlantica & A/S Arcadia (Leif Høegh & Co. A/S, managers), Oslo, and renamed HØEGH TARGET. *1976:* Transferred to Sameiet Høegh Target, Oslo (same managers). *1982:* Transferred to K/S A/S Target, Oslo (same managers) and renamed TARGET. *1985:* Sold to Inter Car Inc. (same managers), Liberia. *1986:* Managers became Barber Ship Management Ltd. *1986:* Sold to K/S A/S Target (same managers). *1988:* Sold to Data Vekst A/S, Oslo (same managers), renamed NOSAC TARGET, and placed on the Norwegian International Register. *11.1988:* Bought by NAL Invest A/S (a subsidiary of NAL), Oslo (same managers), and renamed TARGET. *1989:* Managers became Norwegian Ship Management A/S. *1990:* Renamed

ARMACUP PATRICIA, 16.8.1990   *N. J. Kirby*

ARMACUP PATRICIA at request of charterer. *1993:* Owners absorbed into NAL. *1995:* Tonnage remeasured—25,944 gross, 8,493 net. *1995:* In the present fleet.

NOSAC TANCRED, 19.2.1989   *Michael Lennon*

90. NOSAC TANCRED (1988-1989)/NOSAC SEA (1989-   ) Car/truck carrier
Tonnages: 48,676 gross, 14,603 net, 15,577 deadweight.
Dimensions: 180.02 (190.05) x 32.29 x 13.75 metres. 8.921 draft.
Machinery: 7 cylinder 2S.C.SA Sulzer oil engine by Sumitomo Heavy Industries Ltd., Tamashima.
Capacity: 5,842 cars.
18.2.1987: Launched by Sumitomo Heavy Industries Ltd., Oppama Shipyard, Yokosuka (Yard No. 1142) as NOSAC TANCRED for Astral Carriers Ltd., Liberia.
17.4.1987: Delivered and immediately bareboat chartered to Wilh. Wilhelmsen

NOSAC SEA, 2.9.1995 *Jann Hintz*

Ltd. A/S, Tønsberg. *23.12.1988:* Bareboat charter party and purchase option acquired by Procyon Carriers Ltd. (NAL, managers), Liberia. *30.8.1989:* Bought by Procyon Carriers Ltd. (same managers) and renamed NOSAC SEA. *18.6.1991:* Sold to K/S Benargus A/S & Co. (same managers), registered at Oslo and placed on the Norwegian International Register. *1995:* In the present fleet.

KRISTIANIAFJORD when fitting out as **NOSIRA LIN** at Sunderland, 25.5.1981 *W.S.P.L.*

91. KRISTIANIAFJORD (3) (1989-1993) Bulk carrier
Tonnages: 17,188 gross, 10,486 net, 30,900 deadweight.
Dimensions: 181.31 (188.17) x 23.17 x 14.51 metres. 10.654 draft.
Machinery: 5 cylinder 2S.C.SA Sulzer oil engine by Clark Hawthorn Ltd., Wallsend-on-Tyne.
12.5.1981: Launched by Sunderland Shipbuilders Ltd., Pallion, Sunderland (Yard No. 17) as NOSIRA LIN for Nosira Shipping Ltd. (Bolton Maritime

Management Ltd., managers), London. *26.6.1981:* Delivered. *1986:* Registration transferred to Hamilton, Bermuda. *1988:* Managers became Mountleigh Shipping. *1989:* Sold to J.Lauritzen A/S, Denmark, and renamed DAN BAUTA. *1989:* Bought by K/S Kristianiafjord (Norwegian Ship Management A/S, managers), Oslo, and renamed KRISTIANIAFJORD. Placed on the Norwegian International Register. *1993:* Sold to Vibeke K/S (A/S Eidsiva, managers), Oslo, and renamed FEDERAL VIBEKE, on the Norwegian International Register. *1995:* Still in service.

KONGSFJORD in floating dock

92. KONGSFJORD (4) (1990-1993) Bulk carrier

Tonnages ; 22,009 gross, 12,589 net, 37,675 deadweight.
Dimensions: 180.02 (188.02) x 28.05 x 15.40 metres. 10.842 draft.
Machinery: 6 cylinder 2S.C.SA Sulzer oil engine by Ishikawajima-Harima Heavy Industries Ltd., Aioi.
30.3.1984: Launched by Kanasashi Co. Ltd., Toyohashi (Yard No. 3026) as SANKO CYPRESS for Sunrise Lines S.A. (The Sanko Steamship Co. Ltd., managers), Panama. *27.6.1984:* Delivered. *1985:* Renamed CYPRESS, and managers became Tokumaru Kaiun Co. Ltd. *1985:* Renamed VIRTUE. *1987:* Sold to Jesst Maritime (U.K.) Ltd. (Jollister Shipping Ltd., managers), Panama, and renamed J. SUDA. *1987:* Sold to Jasuda Navigation Inc. (Wallem Shipmanagement Ltd., managers), Panama, and renamed JASAKA. *1988:* Sold to Bantayog Ocean Shipping Inc., Philippines (same managers). *1989:*

KONGSFJORD, 13.10.1991   *Malcolm Dippy*

Sold to Kosmos Shipping A/S (Kosmos Ship Management A/S, managers), Sandefjord, and placed on the Norwegian International Register. *8.1990:* Bought by Salute Marine S.A. (Norwegian Ship Management A/S, managers), Oslo, and renamed KONGSFJORD, on the Norwegian International Register. *3.1993:* Sold to Seamist Marine S.A., Greece, and renamed AYIA MARKELLA. *1995:* Still in service.

SEA PRIDE, 14.10.1994 *J. Y. Freeman*

93. FERNGOLF (1991-1992) / SEA PRIDE (1992-   ) Car carrier
Tonnages: 9,820 gross, 6,592 net, 10,729 deadweight
Dimensions: 155.00 (165.00) x 27.64 x 13.95 metres. 7.802 draft.
Machinery: 12 cylinder 4S.C.SA Vee MAN oil engine by Kawasaki Heavy Industries Ltd., Kobe.
Capacity: 3,150 cars.
25.12.1979: Launched by Kurushima Dockyard Co.Ltd., Onishi (Yard No. 2127) as OCEAN GOLF for Across Ocean Shipping Co. Ltd., Liberia. *21.1.1980:* Delivered. *1984:* Sold to Ferngolf Shipping Inc. (Fearnley & Eger A/S, managers), Liberia and renamed FERNGOLF. *1991:* Bought by NAL (Norwegian Ship Management A/S, managers). *1992:* Renamed SEA PRIDE. Registered at Oslo and placed on the Norwegian International Register. *1994:* Tonnage remeasured — 27,087 gross, 15,630 net. *1995:* In the present fleet.

SEA PRIDE. Note the freshly painted "Oslo"

94. FERNPASSAT (1991-1992) / SEA PREMIER (1992-   ) NOSAC PREMIER (1995-   ) Car carrier
Tonnages: 9,829 gross, 6,604 net, 10,678 deadweight.
Dimensions: 155.02 (165.00) x 27.64 x 13.1995 metres. 7.824 draft.
Machinery: 12 cylinder 4S.C.SA Vee MAN oil engine by Kawasaki Heavy Industries Ltd., Kobe.
Capacity: 3,000 cars.
18.3.1981: Launched by Kurushima Dockyard Co. Ltd., Onishi (Yard No. 2150) as OCEAN PASSAT for Lorraine Carcarrier Corp., Liberia. *10.6.1981:* Delivered. *1984:* Sold to Fernpassat Shipping Inc. (Fearnley & Eger A/S, managers), Liberia, and renamed FERNPASSAT. *1991:* Bought by NAL (Norwegian Ship Management A/S, managers). *1992:* Renamed SEA PREMIER. *7.1993:* Registered at Oslo and placed on the Norwegian International Register. *1994:* Tonnages remeasured — 27,097 gross, 15,630 net. *7.1995:* Renamed NOSAC PREMIER. *1995:* In the present fleet.

KASSEL, 17.8.1995   *Dale E. Crisp*

95. KASSEL (1991-   ) Car carrier
Tonnages: 34,960 gross, 27,903 net, 12,077 deadweight.
Dimensions: 160.61 (172.52) x 29.41 x 11.00 metres. 9.002 draft.
Machinery: 6 cylinder 2S.C.SA Burmeister & Wain oil engine by R. O. Tvornica Dizel Motora 'Uljanik', Pula.
Capacity: 3,555 cars.
27.12.1986: Launched by R. O. Brodogradiliste 'Uljanik', Pula (Yard No. 371) for K/S A/S Fernavant (Fearnley & Eger A/S, managers), Oslo. *1987:* Delivered and placed on the Norwegian International Register. *1991:* Share-holding acquired by NAL and managers became Norwegian Ship Management A/S. *1992:* NAL became managers. *1.6.1994:* NAL acquired 52.5% ownership. *1994:* Transferred to Avant K/S (NAL, managers), Oslo. *1995:* Tonnage remeasured — 34,960 gross, 10,488 net. *1995:* In the present fleet.

96. BRAUNSCHWEIG (1991-   ) Car Carrier
Tonnages: 34,960 gross, 27,903 net, 12,084 deadweight.
Dimensions: 160.00 (172.50) x 29.41 x 20.43 metres. 9.002 draft.
Machinery: 6 cylinder 2S.C.SA Burmeister & Wain oil engine by R. O. Tvornica Dizel Motora 'Uljanik', Pula.
Capacity: 3,742 cars.
13.6.1987: Launched by R. O. Brodogradiliste 'Uljanik', Pula (Yard No. 372) for K/S A/S Ferncaravelle (Fearnley & Eger A/S, managers), Oslo. *2.12.1987:* Delivered, and placed on the Norwegian International Register. *1991:* Share-holding acquired by NAL and managers became Norwegian Ship Management A/S. *1992:* NAL became managers. *1.6.1994:* NAL acquired 49.5% ownership. *1994:* Transferred to Caravelle K/S (NAL, managers). *1995:* Tonnage remeasured — 34,960 gross, 10,488 net. *1995:* In the present fleet.

BRAUNSCHWEIG passing W. H. ADVENTURE, 12.8.1989 J. Y. Freeman

97. LANE (1991-1991) Car carrier
Tonnages: 13,111 gross, 8,070 net, 13,608 deadweight.
Dimemsions: 174.61 (186.01) x 32.03 x 13.19 metres. 9.021 draft.
Machinery: 8 cylinder 2S.C.SA Burmeister & Wain oil engine by Mitsui Engineering & Shipbuilding Co. Ltd., Tamano.
Capacity: 5,408 cars.
Ordered from Hashihama Zosen, Tadotsu as Yard No. 819 by Skibs A/S Silver Line and Silver Fjord, Norway, but contract sold. *22.5.1982:* Launched as MINORU for Minoru Shipping Pte. Ltd. (Yngvar Hvistendahl, manager), Singapore. *20.9.1982:* Delivered. *1987:* Managers restyled Hvistendahls Rederi A/S. *1989:* Sold to Fernstar A/S (Fearnley & Eger A/S, managers), Oslo, renamed FERNSTAR and placed on the Norwegian International Register. *1991:* Bought by NAL (Norwegian Ship Management A/S, managers), Oslo, and renamed LANE. *4.8.1991:* In collision with the Liberian car carrier ASTRO COACH (13,365/80) in dense fog in the Straits of Gibraltar, 7.4 nautical miles from Europa Point Lighthouse in a position 35.59 N, 05.18 W, while on a voyage from Nagoya to Sheerness and Bremerhaven with cars. Fire ensued and she sank about 6 miles south of Gibraltar. One member of the crew was lost.

98. NOREFJORD (3) (1991-1993) Bulk carrier
Tonnages: 23,076 gross, 12,731 net, 38,706 deadweight.
Dimensions: 180.02 (189.97) x 28.45 x 15.52 metres. 11.021 draft.
Machinery: 6 cylinder 2S.C.SA Burmeister & Wain oil engine by Mitsui Engineering & Shipbuilding Co. Ltd., Tamano.
27.11.1984: Launched by Koyo Dockyard Co. Ltd., Mihara (Yard No. 1073) as SUNNY WISTERIA for Ocean Rainbow S.A. (Mitsui-OSK Lines Ltd., managers), Panama. *22.4.1985:* Delivered. *1990:* Sold to Wisteria Navigation Inc. (Shin Yei Senpaku K.K., managers), Liberia. *10.1991:* Bought by K/S Nalbulk (Norwegian Ship Management A/S, managers), Liberia, and renamed NOREFJORD. *1992:* Re-registered at Oslo and placed on the Norwegian International Register. *3.1993:* Sold to Norefjord Navigation Ltd. (A/S Eidsiva, managers), Oslo, on the Norwegian International register. *1994:* Renamed

NOREFJORD, 3.6.1994   Joachim Pein

VIVITA, and management transferred to Ugland Maritime Services A/S. *1995:* Still in service.

99. TRINITY SEA (1991-1994) Bulk carrier
Tonnages: 18,639 gross, 10,508 net, 30,898 deadweight.
Dimensions: 165.00 (174.00) x 26.00 x 14.80 metres. 10.653 draft.
Machinery: 4 cylinder 2S.C.SA Burmeister & Wain oil engine by Mitsui Engineering & Shipbuilding Co. Ltd., Tamano.
24.2.1984: Launched by Hashihama Zosen, Tadotsu (Yard No. 827), as TRIDENT for Tri-Ever Shipping S.A., Panama. *23.5.1984:* Delivered as KOREAN MORNING for Morning Ocean Lines Corp., Panama. *1990:* Sold to Saint River S.A. (Northern Star Shipping Co. Ltd., managers), Panama and renamed TRINITY SEA. *1991:* Chartered by NAL. *1994:* Sold to KLI (Panama) S.A. (Tenyo Kaiun K.K., managers), Panama and renamed AUSTRALIAN RIVER. *1995:* Still in service.

100. TRINITY STAR (1991-1994) Bulk carrier
Tonnages: 13,257 gross, 9,771 net, 23,778 deadweight.
Dimensions: 150.02 (159.85) x 24.64 x 13.62 metres. 9.973 draft.
Machinery: 6 cylinder 2S.C.SA Sulzer oil engine by Mitsubishi Heavy Industries Ltd., Kobe.
30.9.1977: Launched by Imabari Zosen K.K., Marugame (Yard No. 1047), as FAIRWAY for Fairway Shipping Inc., Liberia. *28.11.1977:* Delivered. *1984:* Sold to Argonaut Line Panama S.A., Panama. *1989:* Renamed TRINITY STAR. *22.11.1990:* Grounded while approaching the anchorage at Suao, Taiwan. Refloated soon after by own means, but sustained damage to bottom plates, and leaking badly. Extensive repairs were necessary. *1990:* Sold to Saint River S.A. (Northern Star Shipping Co. Ltd., managers), Panama. *1991:* Chartered by NAL. *1994:* Sold to Calver Shipping Co. Ltd. (M. Odysseos Shipmanagement Ltd., managers), Cyprus and renamed STAR MARY. *1995:* Still in service.

101. FIDELIO (1994-   ) Car/truck carrier
Tonnages: 47,219 gross, 14,165 net, 15,681 deadweight.
Dimensions: 180.27 (190.05) x 32.29 x 19.72 metres. 8.921 draft.
Machinery: 7 cylinder 2S.C.SA Sulzer oil engine by Sumitomo Heavy Industries Ltd., Tamashima.
Capacity: 5,574 cars.
14.9.1986: Launched by Oshima Shipbuilding Co. Ltd., Oshima (Yard No.

FIDELIO, 18.5.1994   *L. Bosschaart*

10101) as NOSAC SKAUKAR for Liberian Paramount Inc. (Norwegian Ship Management A/S, managers), Panama. *1987:* Delivered. *1990:* Sold to A/S Skaugen Car Carriers K/S (Skaugen Marine A/S, managers), Liberia. *1991:* Managers bècame S & C Marine A/S. *1992:* Renamed SKAUKAR. *1994:* Sold to Wallenius Lines, registered under Fidelio Limited Partnership Inc. (International Marine Carriers Inc., managers), U.S.A., and renamed FIDELIO. *22.3.1994:* NAL acquired 35% ownership. *1995:* In the present fleet.

102. Newbuilding (1995-   ) Car/truck carrier
Tonnages: 49,443 gross, 13,548 deadweight
Dimensions: 180.00 (190.05) x 32.26 x 31.04 metres. 8.75 draft.
Capacity: 5,856 cars

103. Newbuilding (1995-   ) Car/truck carrier
Tonnages: 49,443 gross, 13,548 deadweight
Dimensions: 180.00 (190.05) x 32.26 x 31.04 metres. 8.75 draft.
Capacity: 5,856 cars

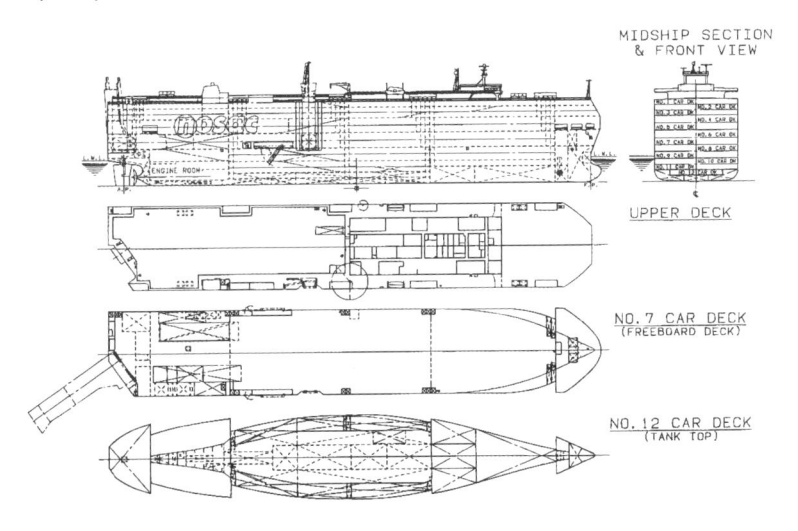

On order from Sumitomo Heavy Industries Ltd., Oppama Shipyard, Osaka, as Yard Numbers 1214 and 1215 for delivery in 12.1996 and 3.1997 respectively.

APPENDIX

During the 1920s, NAL owned a number of harbour tugs, but not many details are available with respect to most of them.

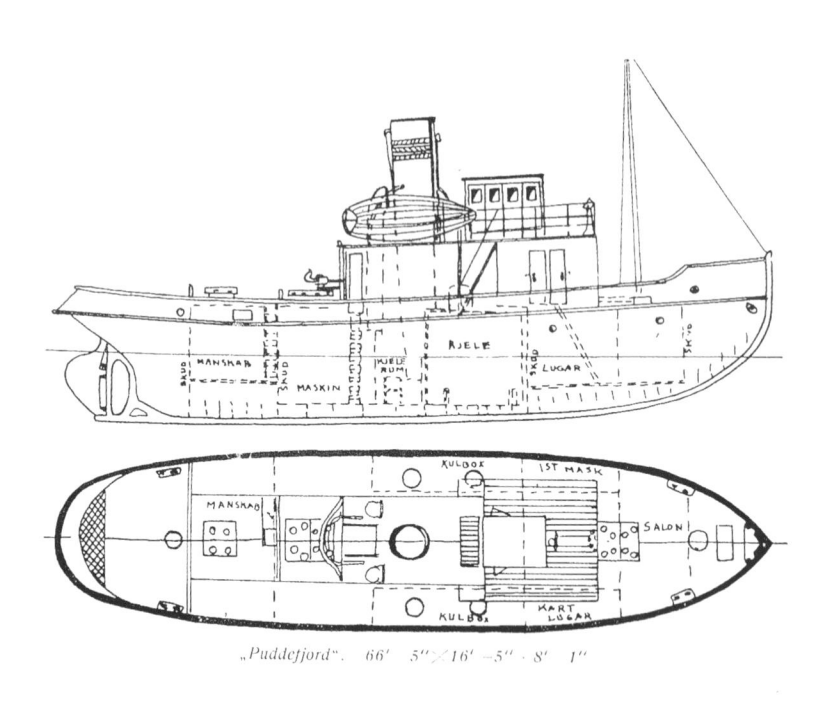

„Puddefjord". 66' 5"✕16' 5" · 8' 1"

PUDDEFJORD

A 1. HAVFISKE (1917-1917)/PUDDEFJORD (1917-1922)
Tonnages: 56 gross, 14 net.
Dimensions: 20.28 x 5.03 x 2.25 metres.
Machinery: Two cylinder compound steam engine by the shipbuilders.
12.1914: Delivered by Pusnes Støberi & Mekanisk Værksted, Arendal (Yard No. 34) as RAPPORT to Einar Stensrud, Skien. *1.4.1916:* Sold to Porsgrunds Kul- og Lægterkompani, Porsgrunn. *8.1916:* Sold to Rederi A/S Orkla (Orkla Grube A/S, managers), Trondheim. *10.1916:* Renamed STOLL. *3.1917:* Sold to Kristiansunds Havfiskeselskap, Kristiansund, and renamed HAVFISKE. *7.1917:* Bought by NAL. *11.1917:* Renamed PUDDEFJORD. *1922:* Sold to Lægterkompaniet A/S, Kristiania, and renamed BRYTEREN. *1936:* Owners' name changed to Bukser- og Bjergningsselskapet A/S. *1949:* Sold to Frierfjordens Iskomité, Porsgrunn. *1955:* Renamed FRIER. *1959:* Renamed FLAKVARP. *1959:* Sold to Johan Naustvik, Haugesund, and rebuilt as a cargo vessel. *1960:* Renamed FØRRESVIK. *1964:* Sold to Øyvind Krogsæter, Molde, and renamed SANDSVALEN. *1974:* Sold to Hjorthamn Sagbruk, Longyearbyen. *1988:* Still in service — no further information.

A 2. BJØRNEFJORD (1917-1922)
1905: Built — original name, builders and owners unknown. *1917:* Bought by NAL and renamed BJØRNEFJORD. *1922:* Sold — no further information.

"Breifjord". 22 m.×6 m 3,1 m.

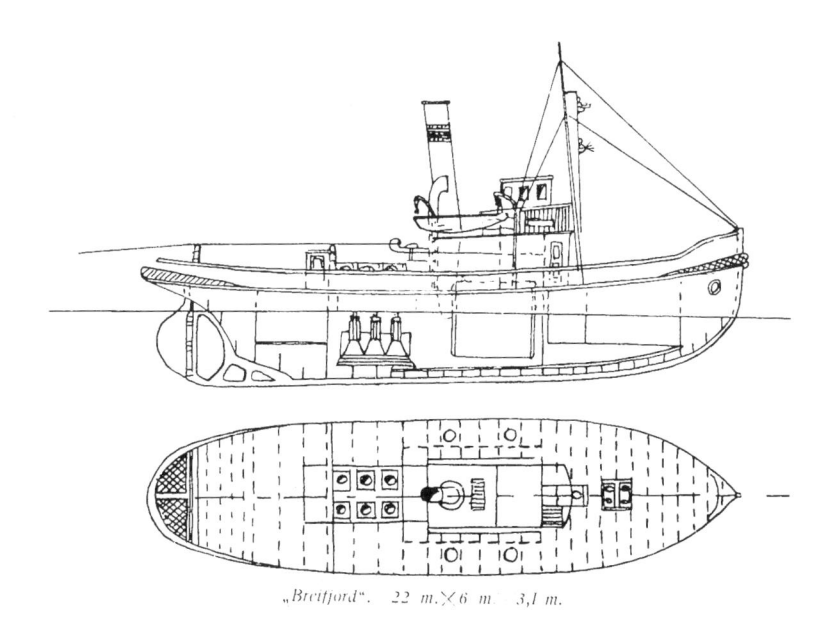

BREIFJORD

A 3. BREIFJORD (1919-1922)
Tonnages: 79 gross, 22 net.
Dimensions: 22.09 x 6.00 x 2.90 metres.
Machinery: Three cylinder triple-expansion steam engine by the shipbuilders.
4.1918: Delivered by A/S Fredriksstad Mekanisk Verksted, Fredrikstad (Yard No. 251) as LIBO to A/S Libo (K. G. Meldahl, manager), Fredrikstad. *1919:* Bought by NAL and renamed BREIFJORD. *1922:* Sold to Lægterkompaniet A/S, Kristiania. *1936:* Owners' name changed to Bukser- og Bjergningskompaniet A/S. *1967:* Sold to Georg Matre, Ølensvåg, rebuilt as a cargo vessel, and renamed ARILD. *1969:* Sold to Ole Leknes, Haugesund, and renamed MIKAL. *1988:* Still in service — no further information.

A 4. VOLRAT (1927-?)
Tonnage: 32 gross.
Dimensions: 14.75 x 4.10 x 2.07 metres.
Machinery: Compound steam engine of 90 horse power.
18.4.1899: Delivered by Lundby Mek. Verks., Gothenburg (Yard No. 13) as VOLRAT to Göteborg Bogserings A.B., Sweden. *1927:* Purchased by NAL. *30.4.1927:* Delivered and taken out as deck cargo to Madagascar where she was in NAL service until given to local interests in the 1950s.

A 5. AXEL (1927-?)
Tonnage: 29 gross.
Dimensions: 14.75 x 4.10 x 2.07 metres.
Machinery: Compound steam engine of 100 horse power.
16.11.1898: Delivered by Lundby Mek. Verks., Gothenburg (Yard No. 12) as AXEL to Göteborg Bogserings A.B., Sweden. *1927:* Purchased by NAL. *30.7.1927:* Delivered and taken out as deck cargo to Madagascar where she was in NAL service until given to local interests in the 1950s.

INDEX

ALTAFJORD		61	LARVIKSFJORD		32	RANENFJORD	1	11
ARMACUP PATRICIA		89	LE NORVÉGIEN		28		2	41
AUDUN		10	LE NORVÉGIEN II		35		3	68
AXEL		A 5	LE NORVÉGIEN III		50	ROMSDALSFJORD		6
BERGENSFJORD	1	2	LE SCANDINAVE		56	SAGAFJORD		65
	2	54	LILLEFJORD	1	9	SEA PREMIER		94
	3	73		2	13	SEA PRIDE		93
	4	75	LYNGENFJORD	1	8	SEA TRANSIT		81
BJØRNEFJORD		A 2		2	34	SKIENSFJORD	1	25
BRAUNSCHWEIG		96		3	42		2	57
BREIFJORD		A 3		4	69	STAVANGERFJORD		12
DRAMMENSFJORD	1	4	MARI		27	STOLT VENTURA		77
	2	29	NOREFJORD	1	14	STOLT VINCITA		76
	3	52		2	49	SUNNDALSFJORD		64
FERNGOLF		93		3	98	TANAFJORD	1	7
FERNPASSAT		94	NOSAC BARBRO		80		2	23
FIDELIO		101	NOSAC BRANCO		83		3	55
FOLDENFJORD	1	15	NOSAC EXPLORER		88		4	71
	2	31	NOSAC EXPRESS		82	TARGET		89
	3	48	NOSAC MASCOT		79	TAVARATRA		66
FRIERFJORD	1	5	NOSAC PREMIER		94	TOPDALSFJORD	1	18
	2	40	NOSAC RANGER		79		2	58
FULVIA		44	NOSAC ROVER		80	TRINITY SEA		99
FØRDEFJORD	1	21	NOSAC SEA		90	TRINITY STAR		100
	2	30	NOSAC SEL		81	TRONDHJEMSFJORD	1	3
GURI		26	NOSAC SKY		87		2	24
HAVFISKE		A 1	NOSAC STAR		85	TRYRIFJORD	1	20
IDEFJORD	1	13	NOSAC SUN		86		2	47
	2	16	NOSAC TANCRED		90	TØNSBERGFJORD		33
	3	60	NOSAC TASCO		88	VIGRAFJORD	1	53
KASSEL		95	NOSAC VERDE		84		2	62
KONGSFJORD	1	37	OCEAN SEL		81	VIKSFJORD		63
	2	46	OSLOFJORD	1	27	VINDAFJORD	1	39
	3	59		2	38		2	51
	4	92		3	44		3	67
KRISTIANIAFJORD	1	1		4	72	VIRA GAS		78
	2	17		5	74	VISTAFJORD	1	43
	3	91	PUDDEFJORD		A 1		2	59
LANE		97	RANDSFJORD	1	19		3	70
LANGFJORD		22		2	36	VOLRAT		A 4

ACKNOWLEDGEMENTS

It was with considerable pleasure that the World Ship Society received the invitation from Norwegian America Line to publish this history of the Company.

A fleet list of NAL by Mr. Per H. Kjærvik was published in the December 1984 edition of "Skipet", the journal of Norsk Skipsfartshistorisk Selskap and this formed a valuable basis against which to check the information available in the World Ship Society's records, and, on occasion, to augment it.

All constructional details are taken from the relevant editions of Lloyd's Register and we record our grateful thanks to Mr. Leslie Spurling and Mrs. Barbara Jones and her colleagues at L.R. for all their help in regard to the ships' histories.

We also gratefully acknowledge the assistance of Rowan Hackman and Kevin O'Donoghue of the W.S.S. Central Record, the Society's Photo Library Team of Cliff Parsons, Jim McFaul and Tony Smith, and the various photographers whose pictures appear in the book. Where no source is quoted, the photographs come from the NAL archives. The Company will be very pleased to hear from readers who have photographs of ships which are not illustrated in the book as they are keen to augment their photographic archives.

Thanks are extended, finally, to Michael Crowdy and Bård Kolltveit for the roles they have played in this project.